The Sacraments: A Charismatic Guide

Chris A. Legebow

DEDICATION

I Thank God for the excellent Bible training I received at my churches in Michigan. I gained understanding of the sacraments and covenants of God as well as knowledge of Christian life.

Chris A. Legebow

CONTENTS

ACKNOWLEDGMENTS

All Scriptures taken from Bible Gateway.com
Modern English Version (MEV)
New International Version (NIV)
King James Version (KJV)

1 INTRODUCATION TO THE SACRAMENTS

Introduction to the sacraments

The sacraments are familiar to denominational protestants and to Roman Catholics. Often, the non-denominational Charismatic or Pentecostal churches do not study the sacraments or do not teach them although most of them still practice them in some form. Understanding the importance and the significance of the sacraments is an essential part of the Christian faith. The word sacrament comes from the Latin meaning a Holy thing. These are practices of the Church introduced by God's instruction that have two parts to them: there is a physical doing of them, but there is also a spiritual significance to them. Faith must be present in the sacrament for it to be of spiritual significance. If there is no faith, there is no sacrament.

I will list the sacraments first and discuss them in more detail.

1.   Water Baptism
2.   Communion or The LORD's Supper
3.   Confirmation
4.   Foot washing
5.   Marriage
6.   Dedication of Children
7.   Anointing with oil: Confirmation

These are core teachings of the Christian Church and essential to the Christian faith. They each have two aspects of them: an outward sign and an inner spiritual work.

Ordinances are traditions of the Church that are done within the church service, and they are different within the different denominations and churches. This book focuses on the Sacraments.

1.   Preaching and teaching God's Word
2.   Public prayer
3.   Praise and worship
4.   Fasting
5.   Giving Thanks to God

6.   Water Baptism [also a sacrament]
7.   Communion [also a sacrament]

Sacraments – Only faith in Jesus Christ and His shed blood can make you Holy. A sacrament cannot make you holy. If there is no faith, there is no sacrament; it is only a ritual.   You cannot be made holy by the sacraments. Jesus Christ died for your sins and rose from the dead. Our righteousness comes through Jesus. Our obedience to God is expressed in our faith and doing of the sacraments. The sacraments do not make us Christians. Because we are Christians, who love Jesus Christ, we partake of the sacraments. Non- Christians should not partake of the sacraments until they accept Jesus Christ as their Saviour.

1 John 1: 9 9 If we confess our sins, he is faithful and just and will forgive us our sins and purify us from all unrighteousness.

To be a Christian, you must literally believe the core of our Christian faith: The Apostle's Creed. There is no outward thing we do as Christians that makes us Christians. There is no outward thing we do as Christians that could make us holy. Our faith in Jesus Christ as Saviour and LORD is what makes us Christians: faith alone.

The only way we can receive the atonement of Jesus dying for our sins is by faith. You cannot sign up to be a church member and be saved. You cannot give money or possessions to be saved. You cannot do good works for it. You can never earn it. Only faith in Jesus Christ saves.

Romans 10: 9 If you declare with your mouth, "Jesus is Lord," and believe in your heart that God raised him from the dead, you will be saved. 10 For it is with your heart that you believe and are justified, and it is with your mouth that you profess your faith and are saved.

The only way to become a Christian is to pray a prayer similar to this one:

Jesus I need you. I have sinned. I am a sinner. I believe you died on the cross for my sins. I believe your blood paid the price for my life. You gave your life as a sacrifice so I could be set free from sin and the consequences of it. Come live in my life. Jesus, I thank you that you are my Saviour. I pray for you to be the LORD over my life. Come fill me with your Holy Spirit. I want to live for you all the days of my life. Amen.

Sacraments can Transform your life

Yes; sacraments can transform your life if they are done in faith. For instance, I will talk about the sacrament of Communion. It depends on where you go to church and your denomination but in many denomination churches, the Christians go forward to the altar area at the church and receive a wafer or piece of bread and a drink of wine or juice. In my particular faith affiliation, we pass out the emblems of bread and juice and each believing member holds on to the elements of communion until all people have received them and we take communion together as the pastor or minister leads us through the scriptures and through prayer.

The Faith is Demonstrated

What you believe as you are taking that bread and juice or wine is most important. Jesus instructed the disciples to do it in remembrance of Him. The Apostle Paul instructs the church in this passage.

1 Corinthians 11: 23 For I received from the Lord what I also passed on to you: The Lord Jesus, on the night he was betrayed, took bread, 24 and when he had given thanks, he broke it and said, "This is my body, which is for you; do this in remembrance of me." 25 In the same way, after supper he took the cup, saying, "This cup is the new covenant in my blood; do this, whenever you drink it, in remembrance of me." 26 For whenever you eat this bread and drink this cup, you proclaim the Lord's death until he comes.

Sacraments should be considered seriously and not done as a habit or a ritual. Each occasion to take part in a sacrament, is a chance to draw close to God in faith believing that what you are doing is giving glory to God. There should be prayer before, during and after the sacrament. During this precious sacrament, we should examine our own hearts. That means it is between you and God alone.

Are you right with God? Is there anything that you have done that separates you from God? There should be no unforgiveness in you. You should be at peace with God and with people as you take part of the communion elements. Please know, if something comes to you that you have done or that you haven't forgiven, immediately repent. In your spirit speak to God and ask Him to completely cleanse you and forgive you. After it, you are welcome to partake of the emblems that represent the body and body of Jesus Christ.

If you are living in willful habitual sin, you should not take part of the sacraments. If you are in sexual sin, or lying, cheating, stealing, hatred etc. you should not take part of the communion table. The Apostle Paul gives strict warning of not respecting the LORD's body and blood. To do it while you know you are sinning is as serious as taking part in the taking of Jesus life. To be guilty of the LORD's blood and body means you are to be blamed for it. This is a most serious consequence.

1 Corinthians 11: 27 So then, whoever eats the bread or drinks the cup of the Lord in an unworthy manner will be guilty of sinning against the body and blood of the Lord. 28 Everyone ought to examine themselves before they eat of the bread and drink from the cup. 29 For those who eat and drink without discerning the body of Christ eat and drink judgment on themselves.

Right Attitude to Enter a Sacrament

Also, the sacraments must be done with faith. I have witnessed this example of what I believe is not a right attitude towards communion. A person talking to his or her friend in Church, chewing gum and blowing bubbles, joking. The person gets up, puts the gum on his or her hand and goes to the front and takes communion and immediately comes back to his or her seat and pops the gum back in and starts joking with his or her friend again. I'm not saying that the person might not be a Christian but to treat the sacrament in such a light hearted nonchalant way is not proper faith in Jesus Christ. Either the person hasn't had right teaching or someone should be correcting that person.

Jesus death, burial and resurrection is the core of our faith. If we do not honour this sacred aspect of our faith, we dishonour the LORD. Our faith should never be casual. Our participation in any of the sacraments must be with faith. They are to be considered seriously as opportunities for us to draw closer to God. Your heart should be longing for God and expecting God to show up as you partake of the sacrament. I don't mean this for communion only. I mean any and all of the sacraments. Faith towards God is inwardly expressed as you partake of the outward symbols. If you are not seeking God in the sacrament, you are not partaking of the sacrament correctly.

It wasn't casual for Jesus to be beaten, and crucified to death. His love towards us isn't casual. God is a person; our relationship with Him should be serious. I am not talking about being solemn in all parts of your life but in all matters concerning your relationship with God treat Him with respect and honour. In the sacraments especially, examine your heart and reach your heart towards God in faith thanking Him that He made the provision for you. God can reveal Himself to you at these special moments in sacraments.

Often, you may feel God's presence strongly. Perhaps God will speak something to you. Most certainly should you yearn for more of God, He will meet you and His Holy Spirit will fill you and fulfill you.

Unworthy Manner

An "unworthy" manner to enter into the sacraments is the warning of the Apostle Paul. He gave this instruction, because some people were doing it. That means we who believe in Christ should be teaching our children and those within our sphere of influence to soberly consider the sacraments or not to partake of them. Rather than take it lightly, it would be best to abstain.

No; you are not righteous in your own self; Jesus is our righteousness, but yes you should be entering in with all serious faith towards God.

Isaiah 64: 6 All of us have become like one who is unclean,
    and all our righteous acts are like filthy rags;

Our righteousness is not earned. It doesn't matter how many years you have been a member of that Church. It doesn't matter if you are the Bishop. The only righteousness is what Jesus Christ applies to you through your faith in His blood shed for you. A worthy manner to enter into the sacraments is a sober faith. O yes there should be rejoicing afterwards. Yes; you may be rejoicing while it is occurring. Before, during and afterwards it is a matter between God and your spirit.

If you believe that anything you have done earns you the right to partake of the sacraments, you lie to yourself. If you give to the poor, if you read verses of scripture, if you say prayers – all of these things are good – they are expressions of our faith; they do not earn you anything with God or give you special privilege to partake of the sacraments. Your righteousness, my righteousness comes by faith in Jesus Christ alone.

1 Corinthians 1: 30 It is because of him that you are in Christ Jesus, who has become for us wisdom from God—that is, our righteousness, holiness and redemption. 31 Therefore, as it is written: "Let the one who boasts boast in the Lord."[d]

If you are unworthy – not taking it seriously and believing that Jesus Christ is your righteousness, you are literally sinning against yourself and God.

1 Corinthians 11: 27-28.... without discerning the body of Christ eat and drink judgment on themselves....

...Unworthy manner will be guilty of sinning against the body and blood of the Lord.

Those warnings of the Apostle Paul are so that we will no sin against ourselves or against God. They are they to caution us to consider our faith sacred and special. If we do not, rather than there be a blessing aspect of them on you, you will be cursing yourself.

I know of people who do not take communion because of a sin in their lives. I respect them that they don't take it lightly but the whole point is, if they got right with God and repented, they could partake without shame or guilt. All you must do as you are about to partake of the sacrament is repent. You truly mean you are repentant – you will stop doing it or if it is a sin of omission, you will start doing it.

Sins of commission – mean sins you willfully did even though you know they are sins.

Sins of Omission – means sins because you should have done something, but you didn't.

Repentance

Repentance can occur in less than a blink of the eye. Your spirit speaking to God confesses the sin and asks God to forgive you – your faith is in Jesus blood to cleanse you. You do not have be excluded from the sacrament if you truly repent.

The Sacraments

The sacraments were made to be an outward symbol of our faith but they are more than an outward symbol. The outward symbol part is there to teach those who are the youth of the Church and unbelievers what Christians believe. It is an outward sign of what we believe for a purpose. It is so those who are witnesses of these things will teach their children and will teach their children until Jesus comes.

O, but there is an inner work of the sacraments. Should you enter into the sacrament with faith, expecting God to meet you, yearning for God, with gratitude of what He has provided for you, something spiritual occurs in your spirit. God's presence comes to you strong. You may feel His Holy presence strongly or you may simply know that He is there with you as an assurance of your faith. There is an inner work to the sacrament. In communion, it most often involves a deep under girding or strengthening of your faith in Jesus Body and Blood given for you. Most often, praise and thanksgiving come so strong in your spirit, you can barely contain it because God has revealed Himself through the sacrament. Yes; I mean there should be a spiritual aspect each time we partake of a sacrament.

Before the Sacrament

Examine your own heart. If there is hindrance to you taking the communion, repent and accept Jesus blood as forgiveness for your sins. Remember how the thief who died on the cross with Jesus, asked for mercy of Jesus and Jesus promised Him life.

Luke 23: 40 But the other criminal rebuked him. "Don't you fear God," he said, "since you are under the same sentence? 41 We are punished justly, for we are getting what our deeds deserve. But this man has done nothing wrong."

42 Then he said, "Jesus, remember me when you come into your kingdom.[d]"

43 Jesus answered him, "Truly I tell you, today you will be with me in paradise."

At that moment of that thief's life, He became a follower of Jesus. Jesus forgave him and promised him life. Repentance can be immediate. It means you were going one way but you stop, turn from the sin and go towards God. It can take one moment. Jesus already died for your sins; you must accept what He has done. Remember Jesus blood shed for you. Receive thanksgiving for Jesus blood. Think about what He said and what He did concerning the sacrament. Most often the pastor or ministers will be sharing scriptures but you also should prepare some scriptures or at least read some scriptures before entering in to the sacrament. The Scripture fixes our hearts on God. God should be the focus of our heart during any of the sacraments.

Really Repent or don't take the Sacrament

If in your heart, you know it is sin and you kind of repent, but think to yourself, I will do it again, you are sinning against God by taking the sacrament. Either truly repent or do not take it. If you do not know how to repent, ask God to help you.

Pray, "God give me a repentant heart. You hate sin. Forgive me for it. Let me hate what you hate and love what you love. Strengthen me so I can live in the Spirit and not in my flesh.``

Do something about it. Cut off the bad relationships. Get different friends in your life. Who you are with determines what you will do and what you will focus on. Get some friends who love God and who want to live for Him.

If there is sexual sin, repent and get married. Don`t make excuses. Maybe you wanted a large wedding etc. but you can`t wait. If you can`t wait, get married. Get the marriage license. Once you get money, invite your friends and family to a party where you celebrate your marriage. Don`t stay in a sinful relationship.

The Apostle Peter

Peter explains to the pilgrims on the day of Pentecost after the 120 who gathered in the upper room waiting for the gift of the Holy Spirit were baptized in the Spirit and started speaking in other tongues and the presence of the Spirit was so strong, it compelled them to go into the streets. They were praising God in their natural language and in tongues and some of them were praising God in languages they had never learned and didn`t know. Jerusalem was crowded because of the feast of Pentecost and some people thought the disciples were drunk. Others knew they were speaking languages from their nations praising God. Peter started preaching to them what was going on.

Thousands of them believed as Peter preached that Jesus is the Messiah. He preached Jesus death, burial and resurrection. Thousands of people were compelled and wanted to know what they should do to be saved. Peter exhorted them:

Acts 2: 38 Peter replied, "Repent and be baptized, every one of you, in the name of Jesus Christ for the forgiveness of your sins. And you will receive the gift of the Holy Spirit. 39 The promise is for you and your children and for all who are far off—for all whom the Lord our God will call."

1.   Repent – get your heart right with God. There should be nothing separating you from God.
2.   Be Baptized – Receive baptism as it is a commandment for those who believe.

Examine Your Heart

If you truly examine your own heart, praying Holy spirit show me if I need to repent, God will honour your faith. It nothing comes to you, thank God and partake. It something comes to you: repent and partake. Don`t exclude yourself by not repenting. God never condemns us. If we come to God with repentance, He never condemns us. The devil brings condemnation not God.

Partaking of the Sacraments

If you partake unworthily there is death. If you are right with God with your heart fixed on God, expect to receive something from God in the sacrament; God will manifest Himself to you if you do it in faith. There is blessing and anointing and grace given to you as a believing member of the Body of Christ should you partake of a sacrament. It brings God`s presence: life, health, strength, anointing. It brings the manifest presence of God. Something happens spiritually as you partake of the sacraments with faith. It strengthens you; it encourages you; it deepens your faith. It`s like spiritual vitamins. It`s God`s best towards you. Receive the spiritual blessings of the sacrament. By faith – it only comes by faith.

Faith Comes

Expect from God and by faith claim the benefits of the sacrament. Thank God for it. Faith quickens your heart. Faith can come as your read the scriptures. Faith can come from hearing the word of God. It can come from your own mouth. It may come through the minister. Receive the opportunity to demonstrate your faith in the sacrament.

Romans 10: 17 Consequently, faith comes from hearing the message, and the message is heard through the word about Christ. 18 But I ask: Did they not hear? Of course they did:

Speak scripture. Think upon the scripture during the sacrament. O yes. Read scripture. Let faith arise in your heart to receive from the sacrament.

Celebrate the Sacraments as A Church

Acts 2: 42 They devoted themselves to the apostles' teaching and to fellowship, to the breaking of bread and to prayer. 43 Everyone was filled with awe at the many wonders and signs performed by the apostles. 44 All the believers were together and had everything in common. 45 They sold property and possessions to give to anyone who had need. 46 Every day they continued to meet together in the temple courts. They broke bread in their homes and ate together with glad and sincere hearts, 47 praising God and enjoying the favor of all the people. And the Lord added to their number daily those who were being saved.

What happened once those thousands of people repented and were baptized is that there were several thousand new Christians in the Church. They gathered in people's homes, talking about God, sharing food and things that are essentials. Their love for one another grew. They became as family. The sacraments are something we Christians do that should knit our hearts together.

They didn't have large auditoriums to gather in – they gathered in homes to praise God. The Church is the people not the building. Thousands of people gathered steadfastly. That means they met and kept meeting. You are a member of the Body of Christ in particular. You are a member of the Universal Body of Christ. You may or not be a member of the local church but you are a valuable part of the body of Christ. There are no non-essential members. All members are important. As soon as you accepted Jesus Christ as your Saviour, you became a member of the Body of Christ.

The early church continued in what the Apostles had taught them. What Peter had spoken. What the apostles taught them about Jesus, they received and believed.

Christian Fellowship

I want to encourage you in your Christian friendships to share some of your time in prayer and in communion. I know some denominations might not like what I am saying. The Bible says they did it in people's homes. I am encouraging you to take communion with your Christian friends. Pray and praise together. Receive something spiritually together.

Celebrating the Lord's presence as Christian friends has brought so much joy to me. I can`t think of anything else that comes close to it. I am referring to praying together, worshipping together and taking communion together in my home. It enriches personal relationships beyond what I can explain. The Bible teaches us that Christ is in the midst of us if we are Christians.

Matthew 18: 19 "Again, truly I tell you that if two of you on earth agree about anything they ask for, it will be done for them by my Father in heaven. 20 For where two or three gather in my name, there am I with them."

Personal celebration of communion is in no way instead of doing it in the local church. I thank God for it in the Church, but also with your Christian friends. It encourages you and them. It releases God`s presence so you can build up each other in the Christian faith. Read the scriptures. Take communion together in your homes.

Communion by Yourself

If there is anything in your life not right with God, repent in your own home. Get the emblems of bread and juice or wine. Make and altar to God right there in your home. I mean you get serious about God and focus only on Him. Repent and rededicate your life to God and take the communion as an outward sign of your repentance and as an inner working of God's presence upon you. Pray `O God thank you for your body and your blood. O God thank you for forgiving me my sins. O God I renew my covenant with you. I thank you for communion. Strengthen me. Lead me. Direct me…'

If you need strengthening in your spirit, take communion by yourself with God. Praise and sing songs to praise God. It will strengthen you. Take communion and believe for God to manifest His presence towards you. Believe that you receive from God.

Serve Communion

I`ve had the opportunity to serve communion to many people. In most churches the deacons do it or the ministers. I am a member of the Body of Christ. I believe in what I am doing. Only Jesus is my authority. I do it by request or sometimes I suggest it. Please if this offends you that a lay person would serve communion, this book is not for you. I believe that all members of the body of Christ may celebrate the sacraments. I know that in my visitations and serving of communion, people were strengthened.

I myself was strengthened. Our faith was built up. Often it was people who couldn't get to church or who were shut ins or in hospital. I served them and it was my privilege and my honour. I know I was ministering strength to the body of Christ. I'm not talking about replacing a minister. I am talking about extra – love to lavish on the body of Christ by serving one another in this way.

You Must be Scriptural

It is a commandment to partake of the sacraments. But if you do not follow the scriptures and do the sacraments not according to the scripture, you are not celebrating the sacraments. Keep it as close to the scriptures as possible. Please know that as I say this, I know there are countries where the people do not have freedom to partake of the sacraments publicly. They must meet in secret. They must hide to worship God. God honours their faith. These people are precious parts of the body of Christ; I must make exception for them. They celebrate the sacraments as they can. We in North America have no excuse for not celebrating the sacraments properly. We live in a free nation. We can publicly gather to celebrate Christ. We can share Christ and follow the scriptures.

2 WATER BAPTISM

Water Baptism – Sacrament

Entering Covenant with God

Hebrews 6: 6 Therefore let us move beyond the elementary teachings about Christ and be taken forward to maturity, not laying again the foundation of repentance from acts that lead to death,[a] and of faith in God, 2 instruction about cleansing rites,[b] the laying on of hands, the resurrection of the dead, and eternal judgment. 3 And God permitting, we will do so.   ,

Hebrews 6 includes the foundational doctrines of the Christine Church. Water Baptism is one of these foundational stones and is also a sacrament. If you haven't been water baptized but you are a Christian, this teaching is prompting for you to obey the LORD and get water Baptized. The purpose of this teaching is to explain why you should be water baptized if you are a Christian. This is in obedience to Jesus and the New Covenant that He brought us through his death, burial and resurrection.

The Old Testament

The Old Covenant is associated with Moses and the commandments that God gave to Moses for the people. The New covenant came through Jesus Christ the Messiah who fulfilled all the laws of Moses by living a Holy life, completely without sin, and who died for us taking our sins and iniquities upon himself. He died; He was buried; on the third day, He arose from the dead triumphant over death, hell and the grave. Jesus is the promised Messiah that is mentioned throughout all of the Old Testament. He fulfilled all the prophecies of the Messiah.

Under the Old Testament, we had to keep those commandments because they were pleasing to God. If someone sinned, he or she must bring an animal (sheep or goat) to the Levitical priests who would make a sacrificial offering to cover our sin. It did not erase the sin or cleanse it but it covered it until the Messiah would come.

Faith in Jesus blood shed for us, washes us clean. God erases the sin as if it did not exist. This is the core of the New Covenant. It is believing in Jesus Christ as our Saviour and accepting the blessings and the responsibilities associated with it. There are two types of sins associated with all humans: original sin because we were born in the human race and Adam and Eve our ancestors sinned against God and we inherit that sin nature from them. Also, there is actual sin. Sin is willfully disobeying God and breaking one or more of the commandments.

Water Baptism not just an Outward sign

Water baptism, like all sacraments, is not just an outward sign of our faith. It has two parts to it: the outward sign and the inner spiritual working. It is a holy action when it is done with faith. Without faith, it is simply getting wet. With faith, it can have deep significance in the life of a believer.

A believer enters into water baptism with repentance. The believer knows that he or she could never be pleasing to God without the blood of Jesus Christ. It is in full obedience to a life of Christian dedication to God. The participant is making a vow to serve God for the rest of his or her life. It is symbolically and significantly identification with Jesus death, burial and resurrection. The Word Baptismo (Greek) means to be totally immersed in the water. The person should be totally immersed in water. John the Baptist was baptizing people who repented and turned towards God. The disciples of Jesus Baptized also.

Romans 6: 4 We were therefore buried with him through baptism into death in order that, just as Christ was raised from the dead through the glory of the Father, we too may live a new life.

Colossians 2: 12 having been buried with him in baptism, in which you were also raised with him through your faith in the working of God, who raised him from the dead.

In water baptism, a spiritual change can occur in the person. It can radically transform a person's life. If it were only an outward sign, Jesus would not command us to do it.

Mark 16: 15 He said to them, "Go into all the world and preach the gospel to all creation. 16 Whoever believes and is baptized will be saved, but whoever does not believe will be condemned. 17 And these signs will accompany those who believe: In my name, they will drive out demons; they will speak in new tongues; 18 they will pick up snakes with their hands; and when they drink deadly poison, it will not hurt them at all; they will place their hands on sick people, and they will get well."

Jesus clearly commanded his disciples to preach the good news but also to water baptize people.

Jesus told Nicodemus that a man must be born of spirit and of water. Being born of water can be our natural birth, but is more than it. It can mean the washing of the water of the Word (Ephesians 5: 26) of God but it also means water baptism.

John 3: 5 Jesus answered, "Very truly I tell you, no one can enter the kingdom of God unless they are born of water and the Spirit.

Believers' Baptism

Believers in Jesus Christ as Saviour should be water baptism. If you do not believe you should not be water baptized. I am preaching a believer's baptism. Although it is proper to bless the children and pray a dedicatory prayer over them, they are not yet believers in Jesus. Believers who with their own free will choose to live for Jesus Christ, should take the next step which is to obey and become water baptized.

Acts 2: 38 Peter replied, "Repent and be baptized, every one of you, in the name of Jesus Christ for the forgiveness of your sins. And you will receive the gift of the Holy Spirit. 39 The promise is for you and your children and for all who are far off—for all whom the Lord our God will call."

There is an association with water baptism and repentance and believing in Jesus Christ and there is an association with the Holy Spirit. Before you had the revelation that Jesus was your Saviour, you were a sinner. You enjoyed sinning and couldn't help yourself. Once you receive Jesus as Saviour, Jesus washes us and cleanses us. Obedience in water baptism is a promise of your life to live for God. Please don't fall for the lie that you must be perfect to be water baptized. Only Jesus is Holy. His blood makes us holy. In ourselves we can do nothing, but Jesus Christ who lives in us, in the person of the Holy Spirit teaches us, convicts us, strengthens us and empowers us to live holy for Christ.

Hebrews 2: 10 In bringing many sons and daughters to glory, it was fitting that God, for whom and through whom everything exists, should make the pioneer of their salvation perfect through what he suffered. 11 Both the one who makes people holy and those who are made holy are of the same family. So Jesus is not ashamed to call them brothers and sisters.

God is able to keep us from falling. The same mighty God who cleanses us is also able to keep us from falling. His righteousness imparted into us makes us holy and blameless. You don't have to believe that you can live holy. That is the main reason many people do not get water baptized. They say to themselves, I don't believe I can live holy to God. Your faith should be that Jesus Christ living in you is able to keep you holy and your faith should be in the shed blood of Jesus Christ to keep you – not in your own strength. No person could in his or her own strength live holy. The good news is that we don't have to do it in our own strength. We can live Holy because God lives on the inside of us and can keep us.

Philippians 4: 13 I can do all this through him who gives me strength.

Baptized

In some places in scripture is tells us to be baptized in the name of the Father, the Son and the Holy Spirit. In other places, it commands us to be baptized in the name of Jesus. Jesus Christ is LORD. I literally mean the words I've stated. Jesus, our Saviour, the Son of God who was born of a virgin, suffered, died and rose again. Christ is the Greek word for the Anointed One. The Holy Spirit is in Jesus without measure. That means He is fully and completely filled with the Holy Spirit. LORD is the tetragrammaton (YHWH) that we translate as Jehovah or LORD – meaning all God the creator and "I AM that I AM". Jesus Christ is LORD. He is one with God and equal to God.

Matthew 28: 19 Therefore go and make disciples of all nations, baptizing them in the name of the Father and of the Son and of the Holy Spirit, 20 and teaching them to obey everything I have commanded you. And surely I am with you always, to the very end of the age."

Acts 19: 5 On hearing this, they were baptized in the name of the Lord Jesus. 6 When Paul placed his hands on them, the Holy Spirit came on them, and they spoke in tongues[b] and prophesied. 7 There were about twelve men in all.

There are strong feelings about these simple truths I mentioned. Some would be outraged that we did not follow the teachings of Matthew 28. Others would be outraged that we did not follow the teachings of Acts 19. Please if this is a cause of offense for you, repent and be baptized in either one so that you may receive the Holy Spirit.

Romans 6: 3 Or don't you know that all of us who were baptized into Christ Jesus were baptized into his death? 4 We were therefore buried with him through baptism into death in order that, just as Christ was raised from the dead through the glory of the Father, we too may live a new life.

This scripture is not only a nice analogy. It is a symbolic but spiritually significant thing that occurs. As you go under the waters, you are baptized into Jesus death and burial; as you rise up out of the waters, you are rising to newness of life in Christ as He arose from the dead.

It should be taught with this understanding to those who are getting baptized. It is our faith in the scriptures and in Jesus death, burial and resurrection that give us spiritual strength. The engrafted scripture can transform your life completely (James 1: 21). As you come up out of the water you are raised to newness of life. If we truly believe in what Jesus did for us, we can completely believe in this transformation of ourselves in water baptism. It is a spiritual thing. You are committing your life to Jesus Christ as a believer. Yes; there is an outward sign. Usually believers are baptized in front of the church. They are witnessing your step of faith. It is not necessary though, remember how Philip preached that Jesus is the Messiah to the Ethiopian Eunuch and he was baptized by the side of the road (Acts 8: 27).

The Inner Work of God

Also, though, there is the part of water baptism that is between you and God. That is the inner working of God in your life. Your faith in Jesus as Saviour is expressed. If you will believe for Jesus the deliverer to circumcise your heart, or cut out the hardness of you towards God, you will receive it.

Acts 2: 29 No, a person is a Jew who is one inwardly; and circumcision is circumcision of the heart, by the Spirit, not by the written code. Such a person's praise is not from other people, but from God.

God promised that He would bring a New Covenant to Israel. He promised to soften their hard hearts (Ezekiel 36:26).

Circumcision of heart

A spiritual work is done on our heart when we enter into water baptism by faith. Enmity or hatred towards God is cut out. The hard spot you never let God in, becomes soft and you wholly want God with all your spirit, soul and body (1 Thessalonians 5: 23). The only way enmity can be cut out of your heart is by faith in Jesus Christ. It can occur in the waters of baptism should you know that it can. The old sinful nature can be cut off and new spiritual life blossom in that area of your life. If you do not believe for it, it will not happen.

Your hardiness of heart can be cut out and it can be replaced with a soft heart or passionate heart for God.

Hebrews 10: 15 The Holy Spirit also testifies to us about this. First he says:

16 "This is the covenant I will make with them
    after that time, says the Lord.
I will put my laws in their hearts,
    and I will write them on their minds."[b]

17 Then he adds:

"Their sins and lawless acts
    I will remember no more."[c]

18 And where these have been forgiven, sacrifice for sin is no longer necessary.

He promised to cut out their hard hearts or the enmity or hatred they had towards God. A person is born in sin because of Adam and Eve's transgression or sin against God. Every person born on earth has this sin nature. It must die so if we are to live in the Spirit. Also, people who sin and keep sinning, get hardened to that sin. They might feel guilt at first, but if they sin and keep sinning that sin. They get hardened like a callous on your hand or foot. That means the hard spot blocks God from that place in their lives.

O, please realize it is most serious. Just because they feel no remorse does not mean they are no sinning. I will compare it to this example.
Leprosy, is a horrible disease. We usually don't see it in North America, but it still exists in some places of the world without a cure. People can treat you but there is no known cure. The most dangerous aspect of the disease is that it kills nerves so that the people can't feel pain anymore. They could touch a hot stove and not know it. Please see, the chances of real damage to the person can occur because the people don't even know it is a danger. God promised to send us hope from being hard hearted in sin.

Jeremiah 31: 33 "This is the covenant I will make with the people of Israel
    after that time," declares the Lord.

"I will put my law in their minds
  and write it on their hearts.
I will be their God,
  and they will be my people.
34 No longer will they teach their neighbor,
  or say to one another, 'Know the Lord,'
because they will all know me,
  from the least of them to the greatest,"
declares the Lord.
"For I will forgive their wickedness
  and will remember their sins no more."

God promised to transform us so that we would not be the same. A person can be baptized in faith believing for circumcision of heart – that means expecting that any part of you that needs to die because it is hard against God – will die. Just as in the covenant with Abraham, all males had to be circumcised, as a sign of their faith in the covenant, God Himself circumcises our inner hearts of any hardness towards God. It includes original sin (inherited from Adam and Eve) but also any hardness of heart that comes through inherited sins or iniquities.

Iniquity

Iniquity is inherited sin that is passed through the bloodline of a family. What it means is that in some families, all the people commit similar sins. If no one repents of the sin, it can be passed on for generations.

Numbers 14: 18 'The Lord is slow to anger, abounding in love and forgiving sin and rebellion. Yet he does not leave the guilty unpunished; he punishes the children for the sin of the parents to the third and fourth generation.'

Inherited sins or Iniquities

You may see that diseases may run in certain families. There are things that can be genetically inherited. Similarly, certain sins, are spiritually inherited, until someone repents and prays mercy for his or her family and all the generations to follow. After you are saved and have repented for your sins, you should pray for the Holy Spirit to quicken to you any iniquities in your family. By discerning of spirits, God can show you the iniquities. You can repent of them and pray for your family to be delivered from their sins. Only God Himself can set them free. Your prayers, can release people who could share Christ with them. Your prayers could release angels who will intervene and protect them. I have known of parents who get an anointed cloth from the prayer meeting praying deliverance for a loved one, who place that cloth in the loved one's room. It is the faith that makes the difference.

If you are not yet Water Baptized

If you are a Christian but you have not been water baptized, I want you to examine your heart as to why. It is not a normal thing to hesitate to obey God once you know His commandments. Hesitation means there is an issue. Jesus commanded us to teach and preach water baptism. This means we should want to obey Jesus Christ and follow his Word. Don't let any lie of the enemy tell you that you aren't good enough to be water baptized. That is a lie from the devil. Jesus blood makes you holy. All aspects of our Christian faith are focused on the Holiness of Jesus Christ and what He did for us. It's not what we can do for Him or what we can give Him. Our best efforts are nowhere near God's standard for complete holiness. Only Jesus is our hope of righteousness.

Romans 2: 22 This righteousness is given through faith in[h] Jesus Christ to all who believe. There is no difference between Jew and Gentile,

1 Corinthians 5: 21 God made him who had no sin to be sin[b] for us, so that in him we might become the righteousness of God.

If you are hesitating to be water baptized, and it is not that you don't believe that Jesus is your righteousness, and you don't even know the reason why but you just can't commit to water baptism, I would highly recommend fasting and prayer. It can be your choice, partial fast or liquid fast, but you should seek God and ask Him to show you why you are hesitating. There may be some part of your life that you must submit to God.

I was Baptized as a baby

My parents were not Christians, but baptizing babies was the thing people did who wanted to show care for their children. I have no memory of it at all. I was prayed for and sprinkled with water as a baby. Believe me, I had no confession of faith in Jesus. I couldn't even walk without holding on to things. I've seen the pictures of me all dressed up in the prettiest dress, holding on to furniture as I walked around the living room. If you were baptized as a baby, you should pray about whether or not you should be water baptized for a believers baptism – immersed in water.

In no way does this insult your parents. They did what they thought was best, but you really had no say about it. The truth is now you do. The Bible clearly teaches immersion baptism for believers.

The reason some churches sprinkle water baptize comes from the early church in Rome who were persecuted for their faith if they worshipped openly. They used the minimum requirement because they could not openly water baptize in public places. A sprinkle of water would represent what was meant to be total immersion. I believe God has much mercy on Christians who can no openly confess their faith, but we in North America have no reason not to be baptized in water. We should not be satisfied with the minimum requirement because of tradition rather than what the Bible states we are to do.

The Waters of Baptism do not make you holy

The outward action of being baptized has no significance if you have no faith. You must believe in Jesus for there to be any significance. Some people believe the sacraments themselves are what makes you holy, but it is not scriptural. Faith in Jesus Christ makes you holy. Obedience to God makes you a scriptural Christian.

God knows we humans need some profound significant aspects of our faith (outward signs) to make the inner working of the Holy Spirit more memorable for us. The sacraments are memorial markers in our Christian faith. They are important. We celebrate them. We respect them. We should treasure them. We should teach them to our children so they understand the significance even while they are children.

Identification with Jesus

You should not enter in to any sacrament without instruction. You should get some teaching from your parents, or from someone at your church. Sometimes, it is taught in a classroom or sometimes it is taught by ministers the day of the sacrament. Getting spiritual instruction as well as practical instruction helps the process to go smoothly.

Think of it as being immersed in Jesus: His death, burial and resurrection. Identify with it and believe that as you partake in it, it will affect your life. You are completely one with Jesus. You are in Christ and Christ is in you. You are stating, my life is hid in Christ. I am one with Jesus in death, burial and resurrection. Jesus is the only holiness for me.

Colossians 3: 3 For you died, and your life is now hidden with Christ in God. 4 When Christ, who is your[a] life, appears, then you also will appear with him in glory.

Romans 6: 3 Or don't you know that all of us who were baptized into Christ Jesus were baptized into his death? 4 We were therefore buried with him through baptism into death in order that, just as Christ was raised from the dead through the glory of the Father, we too may live a new life.

The identification is literal. You believe in your heart that Christ died for you but you also enter in by demonstrating your faith through obedience to God and are immersed in water – into the death, burial and resurrection of Jesus Christ. The identification places you as a participant rather than an observer. Rather than stand at the foot of the cross to see Jesus dying for your sins, you believe you are in Christ – His death replaces your own death. Surely the sentence of sin is death and you and I are worthy of death because of it. You are in Christ – with Him as He died on that cross, as He defeated hell and the grave, as He rose to newness of life.

Fruit of the Spirit

Although we are in complete identification with Christ in baptism, the character of Christ is formed in us as we are changed from glory to glory in the presence of God in prayer and in reading of God's Word. Usually, water baptism is a place of deciding for more of God and pressing into Christ more than ever before. What that means is the person will want to hear preaching, desire to read God's word and pray, seek God and spiritual friends more than in the past. These decisions all focus on Jesus Christ and what occurs is Christ's character begins to be formed in your inner most being.

Galatians 5: 22 But the fruit of the Spirit is love, joy, peace, forbearance, kindness, goodness, faithfulness, 23 gentleness and self-control. Against such things there is no law.

What happens with the believer who dedicates his or her life to God is that he or she becomes more like God the more he or she is in God's presence. The characteristics we would use to describe Christ will be formed in us. Generally, it includes all the fruit of the Spirit and also these qualities: merciful, kind, compassionate, caring, forgiving, giving, generous, genuine. You may not notice it in yourself but others will see it in you. They may comment. Occasionally, upon self-reflection, you will think of how

God has changed you so that the way you used to be either angry or put off, you will now be kind and patient and forgiving. What is occurring is very special. The Holy Spirit is making you more like Christ so that your life can give God glory. People will see Christ in you. They may ask you about God because of it or perhaps you will have an opportunity to witness to someone because they will ask you why you are so positive.

Because Jesus is living on the inside of you, and because you are desiring to know more of God, the fruit of the spirit are more evident in your life. Part of it is you don't do the same things you did before you knew Christ. Part of it is you don't think the way you did before you knew Christ. Your spirit has been born- again. The Holy Spirit's presence in you makes all the difference.

2 Peter 1: 3 His divine power has given us everything we need for a godly life through our knowledge of him who called us by his own glory and goodness. 4 Through these he has given us his very great and precious promises, so that through them you may participate in the divine nature, having escaped the corruption in the world caused by evil desires.
5 For this very reason, make every effort to add to your faith goodness; and to goodness, knowledge; 6 and to knowledge, self-control; and to self-control, perseverance; and to perseverance, godliness; 7 and to godliness, mutual affection; and to mutual affection, love. 8 For if you possess these qualities in increasing measure, they will keep you from being ineffective and unproductive in your knowledge of our Lord Jesus Christ. 9 But whoever does not have them is nearsighted and blind, forgetting that they have been cleansed from their past sins.

God gives us all things for a godly life, but we should be making every effort to add to our faith. The Holy Spirit living in us is changing us but we also should be sensitive to the Holy Spirit and we should add to our faith. It is not as though we could do it without God's help. Literally, it means that God will shine the light on areas of our lives and we will pray concerning these things and get the Word of God on the inside of us by reading it, praying it, and confessing it.

Peace, that passes all understanding, joy, and His godly nature are characteristics of Christ. I read an excellent book by Thomas A Kempis right after I got saved called "The Imitation of Christ". It is a book about being transformed by God to become more Christ like. It is an excellent book, but not everyone may like the early English because the book was written about a thousand years ago. This early saint of the Christian Church had a revelation of what it means to identify with Christ. It means that is

Christ is, so should we be.

Philippians 2: 5 In your relationships with one another, have the same mindset as Christ Jesus:
Who, being in very nature[a] God,
    did not consider equality with God something to be used to his own advantage;
7 rather, he made himself nothing
    by taking the very nature[b] of a servant,
    being made in human likeness.
8 And being found in appearance as a man,
    he humbled himself
    by becoming obedient to death—
        even death on a cross!

Serving

This scripture tells us that we should be made like Christ in our desire to serve. We should enjoy serving and helping others. It should become a part of our character. We should desire to serve God by sharing Christ with others. We should care about people and be quick to give help to people. Because you are a part of the body of Christ, God will speak to you and prompt you to pray for people or to help people. God will place someone on your heart and you will check on that person and encourage him or her and make a difference.

The love you have for people will be clear because you will start caring about people at church in a new way. You may pray for them more or listen to them more because you really care. It will also include non-Christians. Our love for people should be so strong that it compels us to share Jesus Christ with them. They will see something different about us rather than other people. They will see something of Christ in us causing us to make a difference. Our lives should be so radical that Christ living in us lives through us.

We do not do things because we have to, we do them because we want to – we want to show God's love for people. We want to make a difference in our community. We want people to get saved. We want to help people if all we do is plant a seed of faith in them. Because we know the goodness of Christ, we will want to share it with others. Should you speak to someone for five or six minutes, you will hear the most important things in that person's life. Listening to a person and responding with caring will make the biggest difference.

Hebrews 11: 6 And without faith it is impossible to please God, because anyone who comes to him must believe that he exists and that he rewards those who earnestly seek him.

3 COMMUNION

Communion

All Christians celebrate this sacrament of Communion of The LORD's supper. Some denominations do it every service; some, every Sunday; some once a month. Remember that a sacrament has two parts to it. There is an outward sign, something you do and an inner working of the Holy Spirit. It is more than simply a religious tradition. If there is no faith in the spiritual dimension of the sacrament – it has no real value. Communion, is something started by Jesus Christ Himself with his disciples at his last supper with them on Passover.

Passover

Passover is a major celebration of Jewish people. For thousands of years, Jewish people have celebrated the Passover with much joy and rejoicing because God delivered them from Egyptian bondage after 400 years. The Jews in Egypt did not know freedom. Not one of them had experienced freedom. They knew Joseph had been blessed by God in Egypt and they had a hope that the deliverer would come and redeem them as was promised to Abraham. After the last plague on Egypt, the death of the first-born child, Pharaoh let Israel go free. Moses lead the children of Israel out of Egypt at the specific instruction of Jehovah who told them to slay a pure unblemished lamb and sprinkle the blood over the doorposts and window seals.

The blood would protect them from the Angel of Death that would come to slay the first-born living in Egypt. The tradition of Passover includes all the elements spoken by God to Moses. They could not have any leavened bread. Today, we use Matzah crackers made for Passover. The Israelites were to have bread without yeast, to show their escape was quick. They were to have bitter herbs to show their life in slavery was hard. They were to have hard eggs to show how God prospered them and multiplied them. They were to have some sweets such as apples and honey to show how God brought joy to them.

All of Israel obeyed God and their lives were spared. The Egyptians who did not put a lamb's blood over their door, the first born in each family died. It was the death of Pharaoh's own son that caused him to release Israel. He sent for Moses and gave them freedom. There are some Christians who celebrate the Passover but not many. God delivered us from the bondage of sin and iniquity. God delivered us from the curse of the consequences of sin. Faith in Jesus Christ makes us inheritors of the blessings of Abraham. We should celebrate the Passover meal thanking God for what He did for Israel. Our God is the mighty God of Israel.

Jesus gave his disciples specific instructions on how to prepare for the Passover. His instruction is an example of specific prophecy. It happens exactly as Jesus tells them.

Luke 22: 7 Then came the day of Unleavened Bread on which the Passover lamb had to be sacrificed. 8 Jesus sent Peter and John, saying, "Go and make preparations for us to eat the Passover."

9 "Where do you want us to prepare for it?" they asked.

10 He replied, "As you enter the city, a man carrying a jar of water will meet you. Follow him to the house that he enters, 11 and say to the owner of the house, 'The Teacher asks: Where is the guest room, where I may eat the Passover with my disciples?' 12 He will show you a large room upstairs, all furnished. Make preparations there."

13 They left and found things just as Jesus had told them. So they prepared the Passover.

The disciples obeyed and made ready for the feast. They had celebrated Passover with Jesus in the past. They had followed him for three years, It is a release of thanksgiving for deliverance and much praise and involves food and rejoicing with giving glory to God. It is at dinner while they are enjoying the celebration that Jesus speaks these words that have deep significance.

Luke 22: 14 When the hour came, Jesus and his apostles reclined at the table. 15 And he said to them, "I have eagerly desired to eat this Passover with you before I suffer. 16 For I tell you, I will not eat it again until it finds fulfillment in the kingdom of God."

Jesus knows this is the last celebration of Passover he will have with his disciples as a man. He knows that He is fulfilling the scriptures by giving his life as a sacrifice for all people. He knows he is the Passover lamb. He is to be the sacrifice for the sins of people. He had lived with his disciples for three years mentoring them, teaching them, showing them his mission so they could share that Messiah had come. He prayed with Him and lived closely with them for those three years. They had seen miracles including the raising of the dead. It is during the Passover meal, as traditionally celebrated according to what was given to Moses, where Jesus speaks to His disciples. Jesus holds up the unleavened bread and says

Luke 22: 19 And he took bread, gave thanks and broke it, and gave it to them, saying, "This is my body given for you; do this in remembrance of me."

20 In the same way, after the supper he took the cup, saying, "This cup is the new covenant in my blood, which is poured out for you.[a]

Jesus the Passover Lamb

No one had ever said those words before. Only the Messiah or the deliverer could say these words. He was claiming to be the Messiah by saying He was giving his body for them. The disciples knew the Passover celebration quite well. They also knew Jesus was saying something significant in these words but they did not have a complete understanding of it until Jesus died and rose from the dead. He is claiming to be the bread of life. He is claiming that the Passover elements are symbolic of His life given for them. He makes the association so clear so that afterwards the disciples will remember. He even gives them cue words `remember me` by doing it. He breaks the bread and gives it them after saying that the bread is his body.

They were not partaking of the Old Covenant`s Passover meal. The bread was not the quick bread because of needing to escape, but rather they have Jesus words that the bread is his body. That is why we no longer call it a Passover meal – but the body or bread and the wine or juice or blood of Jesus represent our salvation from sin. Jesus is the Passover sacrifice – once for all people. After supper, Jesus takes the cup. He offers them drink from the cup and he says it is his blood shed for them – the blood of the new covenant. Jesus is saying his blood is in the cup. It is not his literal blood in that cup. I don`t believe they understood the significance of his blood shed until right afterwards when he died on the cross and rose from the dead. After he had died, they understood the promises of the Prophet Isaiah in Isaiah 53 of the death the coming Messiah – of Jesus. He makes it clear that his blood is associated with that cup, the cup of the Passover lamb – Jesus.

The Apostle Paul

Later, The Apostle Paul, who had been born Saul, would not have understood the association to Jesus except Jesus appeared to him and revealed himself as the Messiah. Paul had studied the law of the Pharisees and was an expert at it. Jesus appeared to the Apostle Paul on the road to Damascus. It was after Jesus had risen from the dead and ascended into heaven visibly in front of over 500 witnesses. It is after Jesus reveals himself as Saviour to Paul that Paul becomes a passionate Christian and leader of missions in the church. Paul especially witnessed to Gentiles – that is people such as you and I. We were not born Jews. We were without hope, until Jesus made the way for us to be saved. The Apostle Paul was especially used to spread God`s word throughout Greece and Europe and Asia.

God inspired Paul to write letters to the churches as he oversaw them and cared for them and helped to train their leaders in Christian service and virtues. Paul gives instructions to the church at Corinth on how celebrate the Lord`s supper or communion – which is really the culmination of Passover.

1 Corinthians 11: 23 I have received of the Lord that which I delivered to you: that the Lord Jesus, on the night in which He was betrayed, took bread. 24 When He had given thanks, He broke it and said, "Take and eat. This is My body which is broken for you. Do this in remembrance of Me."[a] 25 In the same manner He took the cup after He had supper, saying, "This cup is the new covenant in My blood. Do this, as often as you drink it, in remembrance of Me."[b] 26 As often as you eat this bread and drink this cup, you proclaim the Lord's death until He comes.

The apostle is instructing disciples to believe on the death, burial and resurrection of Jesus Christ in the taking of the body and the blood of Jesus represented by the bread and wine or juice. Jesus Christ lived without sin. He could die as a holy, truly holy with no sin, man of God. He was beaten and abused and died on a cross for no reason except he claimed to be the Messiah. He is the Messiah. He died without committing one sin so that it was possible that you and I who believe in him can be saved. Jesus died to take our place. Jesus died for our sins.

Communion is a symbol of the New Covenant of Jesus Christ

If you take the piece of bread believing that Jesus died and rose from the dead for you, you can life and health and strength in the communion sacrament. If you believe it is more than a piece of bread or bit of wine or juice. It is life to you. There is blessing in it because you remember the LORD Jesus Christ. If you do not believe Jesus is your Saviour, you should not take communion. It is warned against by the apostle Paul.

Luke 22: 27 Therefore whoever eats this bread and drinks this cup of the

Lord unworthily will be guilty of the body and blood of the Lord. 28 Let a man examine himself, and so eat of the bread

and drink of the cup. 29 For he who eats and drinks unworthily, eats and drinks damnation to himself, not discerning the Lord's body.

Examine your Heart

If you do not believe, you are guilty of the blood and body of Jesus. That is most serious. Christians must examine their hearts at the LORD`s supper or Communion. We literally pray, 'God show me if there is anything unpleasing to you'. If God quickens something to you, repent quickly. Repent means to completely stop doing it and turn towards the LORD. Stop the sin and do something for God instead. Replace the negative with something positive.

The scripture says 'let a man examine himself'. What it means is the communion of God is between you and God. No one else should be telling you that you are worthy or unworthy. Only the Holy Spirit can examine your heart. If you pray for the Holy Spirit to quicken you to anything unpleasing to God and God brings conviction of sin – repent. Ask God to forgive you. Receive the blood of Jesus as the cleansing for your sin. If you are willfully living in sin – that means you know you are sinning but you do it anyway- you repent, take communion and right afterwards go on sinning – you should not partake of Communion. You are mocking God's precious blood.

Hebrews 10: 26 For if we willfully continue to sin after we have received the knowledge of the truth, there no longer remains a sacrifice for sins, 27 but a fearful expectation of judgment and fiery indignation, which will devour the adversaries.

True Repentance

Repentance means you were going one way- a way of sin; It means you turn around and follow God. You don't simply stop the sin; instead you do something – you go to God. You press into Christ more than ever before. You cannot simply stop. You must replace it with following God and living a godly life. You must pray to ask the Holy Spirit to show you what to do – how to live Holy. We cannot do it without Jesus Christ. The good news is that we don't have to live without Christ. Jesus lives on the inside of us in the person of the Holy Spirit. You cannot make it in your own will power; it is Christ living in you that gives you strength to live holy. You do not have to be addicted to sin. Jesus came to set you free. Get some teaching on deliverance if there is reoccurring sin. You don't have to be a sinner. Jesus Christ makes us holy. God said "Be ye Holy as I am holy" . It is possible to live holy by the spirit of God leading and directing you and your continual dying to sin and living unto God.

1 Peter 1: 15 But as He who has called you is holy, so be holy in all your conduct, 16 because it is written, "Be holy, for I am holy."[a]

The communion cup of the LORD is the drinking of his blood. What it means is that your faith in Jesus blood, and your remembering of his death for you, washes you and cleanses you from all sin. We take the cup, thanking God for the gift He has given us in salvation. To believers, it is a cup of blessing or a cup of life. To those who are sinning or to those who don't believe, they should not take it at all.

God is Present in the Communion Sacrament

To those who believe Jesus died and shed His blood for you, you receive it personally thanking Christ for salvation, the cup of wine or grape juice is more than just wine or grape juice. You are receiving the blood of Christ over your life personally – you are made holy by the blood of Christ by faith. The bread is more than just bread; you are receiving by faith the full sacrifice of Jesus Christ the Lamb of God who paid the price for your sins and iniquities. Jesus took upon himself the sins of all people so that those who believe would receive the full covenant blessings promised to Israel through Moses and through Abraham.

The Blood of Jesus Christ is our Righteousness

If you confess your sins to God and receive the blood of Christ, and you don't feel cleansed, you must speak to yourself to get in alignment with God's Word. God word clearly says he cleanses us from all sin – that is true whether you feel it or not. There are people who believe in Christ but who will abuse themselves or punish themselves because they believe they must pay a penalty for their sins. This is done because they have not received the word of God that clearly lets us know there is nothing we could ever do to pay the price for our sins. God didn't find out about your sin when you confessed it; God knew about your sin over 2, 000 years ago; that is why He sent Jesus to die on the cross – so you could be forgiven. The only solution, is to accept the sacrifice of Jesus Christ – the lamb of God – who died for our sins.

The way to feel the cleansing of God on the inside of you it is to get that word on the inside of you; the Bible refers to it as the engrafted word (James 1: 21). You get the word of God from your head to your heart by reading it, praying it, confessing it and believing it fully.

1 John 1: 9 If we confess our sins, He is faithful and just to forgive us our sins and cleanse us from all unrighteousness.

2 Corinthians 5: 21 God made Him who knew no sin to be sin for us, that we might become the righteousness of God in Him.

Write the words on an index card, or print them and paste it to your mirror or your car windshield visor so that you see it often. Say it. Pray it and receive it until without a doubt you align with God's Word. God's Word is always true. God's word is always the source; we must come into alignment with God's Word.

What you can Give

In a true communion sacrament, you are receiving the body and blood of Jesus, but you are also offering your own body, soul and spirit as a living sacrifice to God. You cannot pay for your sins, but you can offer yourself each day as a willing, living sacrifice to God. You can give yourself wholly to God. You can become a living witness of the mercy of God. You must do it by your heart attitude, confessing it and living it. Give yourself wholly to God. You must do it by faith believing that Jesus blood consecrates or separates you unto God. You receive new life in Christ, forgiveness of sins and you give yourself to God so that He might live in you and through you.

Romans 12: 1 I urge you therefore, brothers, by the mercies of God, that you present your bodies as a living sacrifice, holy, and acceptable to God, which is your reasonable service of worship. 2 Do not be conformed to this world, but be transformed by the renewing of your mind, that you may prove what is the good and acceptable and perfect will of God.

1 Thessalonians 5: 23 May the very God of peace sanctify you completely. And I pray to God that your whole spirit, soul, and body be preserved blameless unto the coming of our Lord Jesus Christ.

Living without sin

True Christians do not want to sin; they want to live holy. Christians want to live for God. If you want God and sin but also in sin and repentance and sin and repentance – you feel comfortable in this cycle – do not call yourself a Christian. A real Christian is living for God abhorring sin and dying to the old nature. A true Christian desires God with passion more than anything or anyone. God is the number one person on your agenda each day, every day. God 's Word is your top priority. Get in alignment with God's Word. If you are caught in a cycle of sin, repentance and sin – get some help from ministers who believe in deliverance get serious about God. You can be set free.

Deliverance

If you are caught in a cycle of sin and repentance, please receive the word that Jesus Christ can set you free from it. There could be deep roots of sin from iniquities in your family. It is possible someone (an elder or pastor or mature Christian who is living holy) needs to pray with you so you can be set free. You don't have to be in addiction or bondage to any sin. You can fast and pray about it yourself, but if it is a constant stumbling stone in your life, get some mature Christian to pray with you.

There is a teaching my Marilyn Hickey that totally helped me in an area of my life where I was constantly falling and repenting etc. She said to pray " God if I do that sin YOU NAME IT (to God alone) please help me to get so violently ill that I start throwing up and feel like I'm going to die." That is getting serious about ending a sin cycle in your life. If you are that radical for Jesus Christ, He will meet you and you will be set free.

No more sin Consciousness

Once you receive Jesus Christ as Saviour and LORD, don't keep calling yourself a sinner. You were a sinner, but you got saved by faith in Jesus Christ. You are the righteousness of God in Jesus Christ.

Hebrews 10: 2 Otherwise, would they not have ceased to be offered, since the worshippers, once purified, would no longer be conscious of sins? 3 But in those sacrifices there is an annual reminder of sins.

In the Old Testament, the sins were only covered by the animal sacrifice so the people usually felt guilty and knew they were sinners. Jesus Christ has come. He is Messiah. He died not just to cover our sins but to erase them as if they never existed. If God will not remember your sins because of the blood of Jesus, stop saying you are a sinner. What you say repeatedly and think about yourself becomes your reality. Change your confession to 'I was a sinner, but I have been saved by faith through grace of Jesus Christ. I am the righteousness of God in Jesus Christ.'

Hebrews 10: 9 then He said, "See, I have come to do Your will, O God."[c] He takes away the first that He may establish the second. 10 By this will we have been sanctified through the offering of the body of Jesus Christ once for all.

People may say who do you think you are raising yourself up as holy? They believer once a sinner always a sinner. They believe there is a constant cycle of sin, repentance and sin all during human life. Those who know they have been cleansed by the blood, take the blood of Jesus as literal payment for all sin and iniquity. They have been set free from sin, and know it. They won't be saying that they are sinners. If you didn't know this and it is revealed to you, start saying, "I am the righteousness of God in Jesus Christ".

Jesus raised us up to sit together with Him in heavenly places. Jesus made peace for us between God and us. How dare we come against God's word by constantly referring to ourselves as sinners.

Ephesians 2: 4 But God, being rich in mercy, because of His great love with which He loved us, 5 even when we were dead in sins, made us alive together with Christ (by grace you have been saved), 6 and He raised us up and seated us together in the heavenly places in Christ Jesus, 7 so that in the coming ages He might show the surpassing riches of His grace in kindness toward us in Christ Jesus.

Take Communion

Get right with God every day of your life. Each day offer yourself as a sacrifice to God. If you sin, repent quickly. Run to Jesus Christ, repent and take communion even there by yourself in your home. Take communion and start fresh giving yourself as a living sacrifice to God. Don't focus on your sins after you have repented. Focus on what Jesus Christ did to overcome sin, heal and death and any other curse. Receive by faith the righteousness of God. It matters that you associate yourself with the forgiven and the holy rather than the sinner and the unworthy. It is not humility to call yourself a sinner when God says He has made you Holy. It is insulting God's sacrifice.

There have been seasons in my life where I took communion every day. I knew that what I was doing mattered not only to me that day but it had spiritual significance as I gave myself to God wholly each day.

Christianity is not a bunch or religious things. Faith in Jesus Christ and relationship with Jesus sets us free from sin, hell, death and all the curses mentioned in Deuteronomy 28. Faith in Jesus Christ gives us access to the blessings of Deuteronomy 28. Please if you have not read this chapter, do it.

See the start of the promises to Moses in Deuteronomy (11, 28, 30 – if possible read the book of Deuteronomy and claim the blessings for yourself).

Deuteronomy 28:1 Now it will be, if you will diligently obey the voice of the Lord your God, being careful to do all His commandments which I am commanding you today, then the Lord your God will set you high above all the nations of the earth. 2 And all these blessings will come on you and overtake you if you listen to the voice of the Lord your God.

The blessings of the Old Covenant apply to us today should we live our lives wholly to God. Our inheritance of these promises comes by faith in Jesus Christ who fulfilled the demands of the law – the penalty of sin is death. Jesus paid the price so that we could be eternally saved, so that we could be healed and delivered, and so we could inherit the blessings of the covenants.

Communion

As you take communion in your local church or at a visiting church, it is right we should thank God for what He has given us. Usually, in the churches I have been a part of, we worship and thank God with the new song of the LORD – everyone praising God individually and corporately. We should do it – praise God for communion; also we should be using our gifts in the church - praying for each other and ministering to each other. Right after communion, after we have been knit together by the sacrament and could be used by the Holy Spirit to minister to each other as a church body. We should be praying for others. We should be imparting something to others. God could use us through the gifts of the Spirit in our church.

1 Corinthians 12: 7 But the manifestation of the Spirit is given to everyone for the common good. 8 To one is given by the Spirit the word of wisdom, to another the word of knowledge by the same Spirit, 9 to another faith by the same Spirit, to another gifts of healings by the same Spirit, 10 to another the working of miracles, to another prophecy, to another discerning of spirits, to another various kinds of tongues, and to another the interpretation of tongues. 11 But that one and very same Spirit works all

these, dividing to each one individually as He will.

12 For as the body is one and has many parts, and all the many parts of that one body are one body, so also is Christ. 13 For by one Spirit we are all baptized into one body, whether we are Jews or Gentiles, whether we are slaves or free, and we have all been made to drink of one Spirit. 14 The body is not one part, but many.

A Sacred meal

It is not just a family meal that we take together. There should be a remembering of Jesus and what He did for us during Communion. Jesus commanded us to remember him. We must remember that Jesus suffered, died and rose from the dead and that He is coming back again. We should be taking it most seriously. If you know you are not taking it seriously, reread the scriptures that we usually read during lent or Easter. Identify with the Saviour who suffered for you so that you can live holy. It is not just an outward action. Our hearts should be fixed on God with gratitude and rejoicing at what Jesus has done for us.

Forgiven

Let there be no unforgiveness in you. If someone has wronged you in any way, plead the blood over that person and release him or her. Give it to God. Let there be no bitter roots of unforgiveness in you. You don't have to be friends with those people but you must forgive. Release it to God. Once you commit it to Jesus, He knows how to reach that person and perhaps soften his or her heart. You must determine to forgive no matter what.

Receive the blood and the body, remembering what God has done for you. It becomes a cup of blessing. It becomes an inheritance. God gives us the great commission to go preach the gospel. Please consider your communion seriously.

You are a member of the body of Christ in particular. Your life matters. You are part of the body with gifts and talents and your being in the congregation makes a difference. It matters that you live right not only for your own life but so that you might make a difference in the lives of those in the church. You need to live the life of Christ for yourself and for your family but also because you are an important member of the body of Christ.

1 Corinthians 12: 27 Now you are the body of Christ and members individually.

4 FOOT WASHING

Foot Washing Sacrament

The sacrament of foot washing is often not mentioned in charismatic, or Pentecostal churches even though they may agree with it. It is often ignored. I believe that although many people know that Jesus did it, they do not understand the significance of it.

The Roman Catholic Church and the protestant Anglican churches teach foot washing as a sacrament. It is practiced most certainly once a year. Although I am not a catholic, I respect that the Pope purposely shows Christ's example by foot washing during the week before Easter. Also, the Queen is known for her practice of this sacrament. The Queen is the highest ranking official in Great Britain and the Common wealth nations including Canada. It is a sacrament, an outward sign of serving others as Jesus Christ did. There is also a deep spiritual significance to it. Remember whatsoever is not of faith is sin. I am saying a person could do foot washing, with our faith in Jesus Christ and it be just an outwards sign. It could be practiced much more often by true Christians. The spiritual benefits of it will be examined in this chapter.

John 13: 1 Now before the Passover Feast, Jesus knew that His hour had come to depart from this world to the Father. Having loved His own who were in the world, He loved them to the end.

2 Now supper being concluded, the devil had put into the heart of Judas Iscariot, Simon's son, to betray Him. 3 Jesus, knowing that the Father had given all things into His hands and that He came from God and was going to God, 4 rose from supper, laid aside His garments, and took a towel and wrapped Himself. 5 After that, He poured water into a basin and began to wash the disciples' feet and to wipe them with the towel with which He was wrapped.

Jesus kneeling in the lowest position to wash their feet would have been considered an outrage. The highest person was doing the job of a slave or servant. The apostle Peter blurts out what the others were most likely thinking. He wasn't going to let Jesus serve him in that way.

John 13: 8 Peter said to Him, "You shall never wash my feet!"

Jesus answered him, "If I do not wash you, you have no part with Me."

9 Simon Peter said to Him, "Lord, not my feet only, but also my hands and my head!"

10 Jesus said to him, "He who is bathed needs only to wash his feet, but is completely clean. You are clean, but not all of you." 11 For He knew who would betray Him. Therefore He said, "Not all of you are clean."

Jesus speaks and says if Jesus does not clean their feet, they can have no part in him. Literally, Jesus is speaking about their walk – their faith, how they consider themselves and God. Jesus had to wash their feet to cause them to realize that only in serving and giving is there true leadership. Only in Jesus' example because they knew He was their head stooping to serve them in the posture of a slave or servant, could their hard-hearted pride, their calloused hearts be softened.

Christians, we don't like to think of Jesus as a servant. We like to envision him with angels and crowns and glory that he does certainly have, but Jesus was also the greatest servant of all. He gave his all. He gave his life. Jesus was kneeling washing their feet knowing it was the last night of his life. He knew those feet had to carry the gospel with purity. He was praying for them. Certainly, He knew they would face opposition. He poured over them in the cleansing of their feet, or their lives, praying for each one knowing the destiny of all the disciples. He states that truly He is the Messiah, the master, the LORD. He states that if he has washed their feet, they should wash each other's feet. He is saying their hearts should never become prideful. They should remain humble and see each other with value. He shows the place of the servant to be a place of importance in the kingdom of God.

He is living the scripture he has taught them to be the most important commandments. Love God first and with all your being and truly love others as you love yourself. This scripture literally means loving others as yourself. You would wash your own feet. You would give yourself the best. We are to love others with that same love.

The unconditional "agape" (Greek) love of God can love without condition. There were imperfections in all of the disciples. None of them was perfect. Jesus loved them anyway. It is loving beyond all human love, seeing only the best in people. Only unconditional love of God can love others as you love yourself. Only with God living in you as the Holy Spirit can your heart be overflowing with love so that you give your best to others as you would for yourself. Jesus commanded us to love each other the way that he loves us.

Matthew 22: 37 Jesus said to him, " 'You shall love the Lord your God with all your heart, and with all your soul, and with all your mind.'[c] 38 This is the first and great commandment. 39 And the second is like it: 'You shall love your neighbor as yourself.'[d] 40 On these two commandments hang all the Law and the Prophets."

Truthfully, each Christian can confess, that Jesus Christ, Saviour and risen Lord reached down to his or her life, made it possible to understand His saving grace and lifted him or her up to see Jesus as Saviour and LORD. Only by grace are we saved by faith in Jesus Christ. The grace comes from God; the faith comes from God. It is God's unconditional love and mercy towards us that causes us to know Him as Saviour and LORD. Salvation can come no other way.

Mark 9: 35 He sat down and called the twelve. And He said to them, "If anyone desires to be first, he must be last of all and servant of all."

Testimony

I can truly confess I wanted God and was searching for God. My heart was longing to know God but I was searching all different religions and not even the Judeo- Christian God. I would have never been able to come to God had God not reached down and shown His mercy to me by giving me understanding of Jesus as Saviour and LORD.

Dirty Feet

The washing of hands and feet before supper, was usually the job of the youngest or the servants. It was thought to be a lowly task. It was comparable to the task of cleaning a toilet. It is a job no one wants to do but it must be done. Usually, upon getting together for an important celebration such as Passover, the washing of the hands and feet would have been done before they sat together at dinner. Some Biblical scholars believe that the disciples reclined while dining. How much more important was the necessity of washed hands and feet.

They did not have closed shoes or boots as we do today. They wore sandals. There were only paved roads where Rome had built them. Most the streets were dirt and the animals and people used the streets. They had muddy feet, dirty feet, gritty feet. There were no street cleaners as we have today. Animal waste, garbage, raw sewage would have been normal. Should there be water, there was mud. The feet of the disciples would not be clean. They travelled everywhere by walking. It was not just a ritual cleansing it was a sanitary cleansing for hygiene.

If they did not wash their hands and feet, the germs from the day's dirt and waste would have not only polluted them spiritually but also it would have been unhygienic. Foot washing was the lowest job. It meant going from person to person, literally scrubbing the person's feet and drying them with a towel.

Giving the Foot washing

Jesus who was the Master, their teacher, the Messiah, the LORD stooped to the position of servant. He willingly kneeled to cleanse their feet. The highest rank lowered himself to do what the disciples would not do. In fact, the disciples had been recently arguing among themselves who was the greatest disciple. They were considering earthly ranking and religious prominence. Jesus had to correct their ignorance of true leadership by his example and teaching. Jesus was the guest of honour at the Passover feast. The disciples should never have gone to the Passover table without washed hands and feet. No one among the disciples, believed himself to be in the lowest position to do the dirty lowly job. The minimum thing they could have done is hire a servant to do the task.

Jesus the Standard

Prophetically, Jesus is the Lamb of God with them. It is at this very Passover feast that Jesus reveals the mystery of His body in the bread and His blood in the wine. Jesus is speaking to them and imparting into them what he wants them to remember after he is gone. He reveals that the Passover lamb is really his life given for them. He reveals that his blood is shed for them. He is setting an example of the most important truths that He has taught them for the past three years. He is the LORD and master but kneels the lowest servant to wash the disciples' feet.

Luke 22: 24 There was also rivalry among them concerning which of them was to be counted the greatest. 25 He said to them, "The kings of the Gentiles exercise lordship over them, and those who exercise authority over them are called benefactors. 26 But you are not so. Instead, let him who is greatest among you be as the younger, and he who rules as he who serves. 27 For who is greater: he who sits at the table, or he who serves? Is it not he who sits at the table? But I am among you as He who serves.

Matthew records that even the mother of James and John wanted to give them a high position in heaven. She makes the request of Jesus. Both James and John quickly say they can keep the model of Jesus. They do not hesitate to say they can drink from the same cup of Jesus not understanding what it would mean. Their words proved true because both of them were martyred for their faith in Jesus.

Matthew 20: 20 Then the mother of Zebedee's sons came to Him with her sons. And kneeling before Him, she asked for a certain thing.

21 He said to her, "What do you want?"

She said to Him, "Grant that these two sons of mine may sit, one at Your right hand and one at Your left, in Your kingdom."

22 But Jesus answered, "You do not know what you are asking. Are you able to drink from the cup that I am to drink, and to be baptized with the baptism that I am baptized with?"

They said to Him, "We are able."

23 He said to them, "You will indeed drink from My cup and be baptized with the baptism that I am baptized with. But to sit at My right hand and at My left is not Mine to grant, but it is for those for whom it is prepared by My Father."

24 When the ten heard it, they were moved with indignation against the two brothers. 25 But Jesus called them to Him and said, "You know that the rulers of the Gentiles lord it over them, and those who are great exercise authority over them. 26 It shall not be so among you. Whoever would be great among you, let him serve you, 27 and whoever would be first among you, let him be your slave, 28 even as the Son of Man did not come to be served, but to serve and to give His life as a ransom for many."

Philippians 2: 5 Let this mind be in you all, which was also in Christ Jesus,
 6 who, being in the form of God,
   did not consider equality with God something to be grasped.
7 But He emptied Himself,
   taking upon Himself the form of a servant,
   and was made in the likeness of men.
8 And being found in the form of a man,

He humbled Himself
and became obedient to death,
   even death on a cross.
9 Therefore God highly exalted Him
and gave Him the name which is above every name,
10 that at the name of Jesus every knee should bow,
   of those in heaven and on earth and under the earth,
11 and every tongue should confess that Jesus Christ is Lord,
   to the glory of God the Father.[a]

Servant

As Jesus kneeled making of himself a servant, washing his disciples' feet, praying blessings over them, knowing they were the only ones who would carry the gospel to all the earth, so does the servant in the foot washing take this posture of servant. Those disciples had to be able to live all their lives giving the gospel to the people. He knew they were the hope for all of humans knowing about the truth of Christ and testifying of what they had seen and done living with Jesus throughout the three years of his ministry.

The person who washes feet, must consider himself or herself to be in the posture of a servant. It is a direct identification with Jesus Christ. It is acknowledging that God is the highest. It is a willful humbling of self to show the glory of God. Although it is an outward act, it also has spiritual significance and can bring a deep humility to the person washing the feet of his brother or her sister. Men should be with men; women should be with woman; married couples could be together.

Today at a foot washing, some disinfectant is in the water. People clean themselves and do not come to a foot washing with dirty feet. As you kneel in prayer, you gently wash the warm water over the person's feet and pray blessing over the person. You could be praying scripture or a prayer as it comes to you. You should be thanking God for the person whose feet you are washing and washing his or her feet as though it were Jesus Christ Himself. Should you have this correct attitude, and pray in English and in tongues over the person, your heart will become soft like warm wax. Praise and worship will bubble forth from your innermost being. You may be moved by the Holy Spirit to prophetically pray over the person.

Receiving the Foot Washing

There are some Christians who agree that Jesus did it and are not against it, that do not practice it. Jesus clearly states that He is our example and we ought to wash each other's feet and serve and love one another as Jesus served and loved us. There is promise in Jesus words that we would be blessed if we would do it. If you receive a foot washing but do not receive it in faith as though Jesus Christ Himself is washing your feet, you will not receive the benefits of it. You must receive it as though the Christian washing your feet, is as Jesus Christ kneeling in front of you to serve you. There is a receiving part. You must accept the blessings the person is praying over you.

John 13: 12 So when He had washed their feet, and put on His garments, and sat down again, He said to them, "Do you know what I have done to you? 13 You call Me Teacher and Lord. You speak accurately, for so I am. 14 If I then, your Lord and Teacher, have washed your feet, you also ought to wash one another's feet. 15 For I have given you an example, that you should do as I have done to you. 16 Truly, truly I say to you, a servant is not greater than his master, nor is he who is sent greater than he who sent him. 17 If you know these things, blessed are you if you do them.

The Feet

Not only did the disciples' feet get dirty, they got calloused. They got hardened. They might have scrapes or bruises because of pebbles etc. Their feet were often neglected. The shoes I am wearing right now are really comfortable. They have full support and cushion. I could walk in them all day and I often choose to. Those sandals did not have supports or cushions. They were mostly flat leather. With a new pair of shoes, the leather was stiff and firm but they would eventually be worn into the pattern of the wearer's foot as he or she wore them constantly. Leather shoes do stretch with wear. Usually callouses form on your feet because of the leather. They did not pamper their feet with pedicures like people do today. These were ordinary fisherman and non- dignitaries. They had to clean themselves and care for themselves.

The Romans would have had servants or slaves who attended to them in the Roman baths that were beautiful, anointed with oil and cared for. The Jews had none of that. There are people who for religious reasons will not show their feet. They believe it is shameful to show them. Feet is used though out the Bible with different meanings. In this instance, it is not only referring to the literal feet but to the walk of the person or the person who evangelizes. The walk of a person matters tremendously. The person should not only preach the good news but be living a life that shows he or she walks in line with the word or lives the word by example.

Isaiah 52: 7 How beautiful upon the mountains
   are the feet of him who brings good news,
who proclaims peace,
   who brings good news of happiness,
   who proclaims salvation,
who says to Zion,
   "Your God reigns!"

In some passages of Elizabethan English "feet" is used as a word for sex or sexual organs. To uncover your feet would be considered being naked. I want to refer to the word feet as the identity of the person. Feet being an example of who the person is and how that person lives. It does have to do with sex, because to walk uprightly means that you are sexually pure without sin. The hands and the feet were washed before meals. This is symbolic of keeping pure.

Testimony

I want to tell you about my first foot washing because it was tough on me. I did not want to do it. I was completely hesitant. I had never seen it, except in movies about Jesus. I was hoping to get out of it. I got the teaching on it. It touched my heart. I was praying 'O God don't let there be any calloused hard spots in my life. I want to walk pure. I want to live holy. I want the truth of the gospel to shine though me.' I wanted my heart to be soft. I wanted to be forgiving and giving. I wanted to be a servant who could love my brothers and sisters in Christ with the love of God. I wanted my walk with God to be straight and upright. I wanted my feet, my walk, to show God's glory not be a stumbling stone to anyone observing me so that Jesus could be magnified.

I wanted people who saw my life, to see the character of Christ. I believe in foot washing as a humbling of self and in obedience to Christ's example. My first foot washing was so tough on me. My teacher, who loved me and taught me and cared for me, a woman of prominence, kneeled with a basin of warm water and prayed over me. She was praying blessings and scriptures over me that Christ would use me to preach the gospel. She prayed blessings on me as if I were her own daughter. It was so humbling for me. I began crying and praying realizing that it was Jesus Christ using her to wash my feet. I realized that it was not just an outward symbol. My inner most being was being softened. In the foot washing, all are equal. It is both a member of the Body of Christ receiving, and a member of the body of Christ giving. No one is higher than the other. It stirred my heart so much that it made me want to wash someone else's feet. I knew if my teacher, who had taught me for nine months could kneel and wash my feet, I could wash feet.

I believe we as Christians should celebrate this sacrament, all of us. I believe it should be at minimum once a year. We need to do it. It will stop bickering and arguing. It will stop pride. You cannot stay proud while someone is loving you with the love of Christ washing your feet and praying blessings over you. You cannot stay proud kneeling at someone's feet and praying blessings for him or her thanking God for the person, praying that God will use the person and keep pride.

It is not the water alone, it is the humility of having someone praying over you with such intimate love as Jesus Himself. It is you praying from the Spirit over a person that causes your spirit to be overflowing with the love of Christ towards the person. Pray that God will bless and use the person. Pray that God will keep the person in faith, walking uprightly. Pray that God will bless the person in every area of life. Pray for the person as though you would pray for yourself.

Enmity

If there is any hatred, unforgiveness or hard headed ness towards God or towards a person, you will not be able to wash feet without having it released. Speaking unkind words, gossip or negative things is hatred; it is enmity. Any hatred will be revealed and you will repent as you are washing the person's feet, considering the person as you would your most intimate self. There may be tears and crying as you realize perhaps a fleshly thing you had thought about the person whose feet you are washing. It will completely heal any relationship because if you give yourself wholly to do it, you will be giving to the other person blessings you would pray in all areas of life. Humility drives the devil out of the church. Should Christians live as Jesus in obeying and keeping this sacrament, no gossip, negative speaking etc. will stay in the church.

Foot washing can bring deep healing to relationships. I knew of a married couple who would not let a day go by without making up. If they were arguing about something, they would get a basin of water and they both would wash each other's feet and pray over the spouse blessings. Any pride or self-righteousness cannot stay as you believe you are washing the feet of a member of the Body of Christ. What it does is cause each person to repent and to thank God for his or her spouse rather than argue. It brings healing to relationships. Humility and serving are mighty weapons of the Christian Church.

Sure, there are other ways to serve people to let them know you value them and care for them. But Foot washing is unique. Jesus did it as an example to us. He told us to do it. I don't believe it's a coincidence for God to use this simple humble act of praying and washing feet that brings healing into relationships and strengthens the respect and love each member of the Body of Christ has for each other.

I don't believe the Pope does it for no reason. I don't believe the Queen does it for no reason. It is in direct obedience to Jesus Christ that we take part in a foot washing. It is because Jesus said we would be blessed if we both believed and practiced it. Getting down, washing someone's feet is a way to show the love of Christ. You hold the person's feet whether are not there are callouses, and you pray a blessing. Whether or not there is a deformity, you pray a blessing; even if one nail is misshapen, you pray a blessing. You pray over the person, knowing God values that person and gave his life for that person.

Do it

I am advocating that you incorporate foot washing into your youth retreats or couples' meetings or Sunday school classes. I am saying it will release a blessing if you do it with humility and sincerity and faith. Separate the men from the women unless they are married.

Use warm water with disinfectant. As you wash the water over the person's foot, pray that God would financially, physically and spiritually bless the person. Pray that God would use the person to bring the good news of the gospel. There should be worship and praise during the foot washing as well as prayers in English and often God uses people to pray in tongues also.

5 MARRIAGE

Marriage Sacrament

Marriage is a sacrament. It is more than an agreement. It is also a covenant that people make with each other and with God. There is an action or obedience part that we do but it has spiritual significance. God hates divorce. Marriage is the ceremony of making vows or promises to a person and to God to keep these vows throughout both their lives. Although permission for divorce was given to Moses to give to Israel, it is not God's best choice for people.

Matthew 19: 8 He said to them, "Moses, for the hardness of your hearts, permitted you to divorce your wives, but from the beginning it was not so. 9 But I say to you, whoever divorces his wife, except for sexual immorality, and marries another, commits adultery. And whoever marries her who is divorced commits adultery."

Covenant Aspect of Marriage

Often people do not want to make such serious commitments so they simply live together or have prenuptial agreements. These agreements are based on what should happen should they divorce. Such agreements imply that the people will stay together only as long as they both want it that way. The covenant aspect of marriage almost is never emphasized. In the book of God of Covenant: God's relationship with Man, I describe in more detail the making of a covenant with someone. It usually meant the shedding of blood of both parties making the covenant. Each person vows to care for the other until death. It is more serious than a treaty or promise. It is promised with the life blood of each person, who are in agreement that should the other person need assistance or help, the other will come to defend him or die trying to.

Marriage is mentioned by God referring to Adam and Eve. Eve was created as a companion for Adam, so he wouldn't be alone. They were created as equals. There are so many excellent teachings I could recommend to you. For instance, Eve was created from Adam's rib – from his side, meaning she was not beneath him or above him. They were equal. Adam would have someone to love and speak with and they were commanded to multiply. God wanted them to have as many children as possible. Sex was God's idea. It is meant to be pleasurable. God wanted people to fill all the earth.

Genesis 2: 24 Therefore a man will leave his father and his mother and be joined to his wife, and they will become one flesh.

After the flood, Noah and his family are given the same commandment to replenish the earth by multiplying. God wanted there to be many people on earth. Marriage was the ordained way of two people joining together to live as one family.

Matthew 19: 4 He answered, "Have you not read that He who made them at the beginning 'made them male and female,'[a] 5 and said, 'For this reason a man shall leave his father and mother and be joined to his wife, and the two shall become one flesh'[b]? 6 So they are no longer two, but one flesh. Therefore what God has joined together, let no man put asunder."

The Joining

The words used indicate a coming together of lives. They both agree their lives will be lived together. A person should not lightly enter into such an agreement with any person let alone God Himself. In Christian marriage, God is welcomed and present in the ceremony. The two people are not only making their vows to one another but also to and with God. Such a commitment is sacred. It is the joining of two lives for the glory of God with God as the witness. It literally means they ask God to be in the midst of the marriage. It means both the man and the woman respect God as the leader of the home. They agree to live according to God's Word and to honour each other with their words, actions and lives for all of their lives. God as the head of the home means the Word of God is honored above feelings or disagreements. Both of them, agree to keep God as the center of their marriage.

Ecclesiastes 4: A threefold cord is not quickly broken.

Two people can go to almost any place to arrange for a marriage certificate, without a ceremony and without inviting God into the midst of the marriage. They can focus on their verbal agreement with each other and ignore God or leave God out of it. The relationship is without the presence of God. Two people who make an agreement together can give their best. The man could give 100%. The woman could give 100%. Some days though, perhaps the man can only give 60% towards the marriage because of circumstances. The woman would have to give herself 100% but there would still not be harmony in the home. She would be living giving and giving, all one sided. The same is also true concerning the woman. Perhaps, she could only give 70% effort towards their marriage. The man could give 100% but it wouldn't be enough for their relationship.

If God is in the marriage, God always gives 100%. God never gives less. Sometimes, He gives more. He can strengthen the man or the woman supernaturally so that the marriage is smooth no matter what should occur. God's presence both in their hearts and at the center of their marriage ensures that they are built up, encouraged and strengthened. God should be the head of the relationship and the head of the home.

Living Together without Marriage

Some people believe they want to "try" the relationship and live together before they get married. It feels like a marriage almost. The truth is they have not made a true commitment. If you want to live with someone and have intimate relations with that person, you should marry. If you once knew God, and are living with someone, you should marry – even if it is only getting that people of paper. It becomes official in your country and you have made a serious commitment.

I know that weddings can be expensive, especially should you have a church wedding with dinner. The point is you could do it economically if you spoke with a pastor and got the congregation to help you. I have known several young couples who had been living together but came back to our church to marry and to rededicate their lives to God because they wanted their children to be Christians. Our church would usually host a party for them. People would bring desserts and salads and there would be someone volunteer to cook meat. It was not as fancy as a big hall with a live band, but it was a church family that was forgiving and accepting, welcoming them to return. It is important that it be done publicly. You can invite your friends and family to witness the marriage. This is the best possible choice. It shows a sincere desire to make God the center of the home. It should be in a church that you go to.

There are people who will get married in a church and pay for the service but never attend the church. They rent the hall; they rent the preacher. They do not make a commitment to the church. I have known of other people, who are not living for God but believe it is important to get married in a church.

Prerequisites for Marriage

Many churches offer Bible classes before marriage. Some make it mandatory. I believe it is an excellent way of giving the people teaching on the Biblical view of marriage. I also believe it should be essential that the people know their life's callings and their spiritual giftings before they marry. Often the couple have complimentary gifts. For instance, he may be a servant and she may be a teacher. Together they are a mighty witness for God. There should be spiritual instruction given to the couple as well as practical Biblical teaching.

Marriage is a most serious commitment. In the Old Testament, a man could not be called into the army if he recently married. He had to stay at home for one year before he could enlist. A man could not make other commitments within that first year of marriage.

Deuteronomy 24: 5 When a man has taken a new wife, he shall not go out to war or be charged with any business; he is to be free at home one year, and must bring joy to his wife which he has taken.

The new testament mentioning of marriage does not change from God's original speaking to Moses. The husbands and wives are to respect and honour each other in their relationship with God and with each other. Jesus is the example given. Just as Christ the head and Saviour of the Church, suffered and died to redeem His bride, the Church, so should a man love his wife. The husband should be willing to lay down his life to protect and care for his wife. The wife should submit to her husband. I know the word 'submit' releases all kinds of groanings in both women and men. As a single person, you submit to God and your parents. Submit is not a negative word. It means you agree with them

Ephesians 5: 22 Wives, be submissive to your own husbands as unto the Lord. 23 For the husband is the head of the wife, just as Christ is the head and Savior of the church, which is His body. 24 But as the church submits to Christ, so also let the wives be to their own husbands in everything.

A person is never to submit to ungodly treatment by his or her spouse. A person is not to submit to abuse of any kind. A person is not to submit to anything less than Jesus' example of someone who lays down his life to care for his spouse. Jesus ransomed His Bride, the Church, through His love that compelled him to suffer, die and rise from the dead so we could be free from sin and its curse. Jesus is returning to earth one day soon; He is coming as a Bridegroom for His Bride, the Church. God compares the most sacred relationship we have with our Saviour and the hope of His return to a marriage. That means God considers marriage to be sacred. In both living for Jesus Christ and living in a marriage, the two become one. We are to become one with God for all of eternity.

Marriage is spiritual

If you are married to the right person, God will speak to that person concerning you. If you do not know it is the right person, you should never marry that person. God can give words of wisdom, words of knowledge and words of prophecy concerning your life to your spouse. That is not only one way. I know many women who God has spoken to and given spiritual wisdom to speak to their husbands because God sees the marriage as one family unit. The husband is to love his wife as he loves himself. That means he will do everything possible to give the best and the choicest to his wife. He would care about her desires as well as her gifts.

Ephesians 5: 25 Husbands, love your wives, just as Christ also loved the church and gave Himself for it, 26 that He might sanctify and cleanse it with the washing of water by the word, 27 and that He might present to Himself a glorious church, not having spot, or wrinkle, or any such thing, but that it should be holy and without blemish. 28 In this way men ought to love their wives as their own bodies. He who loves his wife loves himself. 29 For no one ever hated his own flesh, but nourishes and cherishes it, just as the Lord cares for the church. 30 For we are members of His body, of His flesh and of His bones. 31 "For this reason a man shall leave his father and mother and shall be joined to his wife, and the two shall be one flesh."[a] 32 This is a great mystery, but I am speaking about Christ and the church. 33 However, let each one of you love his wife as himself, and let the wife see that she respects her husband.

Love for your wife

One of the best descriptions of a husband's love for his wife that I have heard is Mahesh Chavda speak about God dealing very seriously with him about not only letting his wife explore her gifts and talents but encouraging her to use her gifts and talents. He wept as he said God showed him how much God loved her and her spiritual growth was a top priority. He caused him to change in how he saw her. He should pray for her not only with her. She should pray for him and with him. In this way, they will be honouring God and each other.

The man and the woman should encourage and strengthen each other. In this scripture both the husband and wife are commanded to submit to each other. There is equality in their relationship. There is the promise that neither the husband nor the wife would treat the other less than his or herself. A wise woman knows her husband cares for her spiritually and she should listen to what he is speaking to her. A wise husband knows that his wife has special insight and care for him like no other person on earth. They are made to complement each other as a whole.

Ephesians 5: 20 Give thanks always for all things to God the Father in the name of our Lord Jesus Christ, 21 being submissive to one another in the fear of God.

You are Complete in Christ

I want to come against the lie that the woman completes the man or the man completes the woman. You are not a half. If you are only half a person, you do not know Jesus Christ. If you get married so someone will complete you, you will never be happy. No person on earth can complete you. Only God can fill you so you are complete. God living in us completes us.

Colossians 2: 9 For in Him lives all the fullness of the Godhead bodily. 10 And you are complete in Him, who is the head of all authority and power.

You should marry because you believe God has brought that person into your life and that you would be complimentary to each other, helping each other and strengthening each other. You should marry because you believe that person would be a good parent to your children. You should know without a doubt the person respects and honours and cherishes you. Certainly, there will be physical attraction; there will be spiritual attraction etc. Husbands and wives should build each other up spiritually. They should speak and pray scripture over each other.

Ephesians 5: 26 that He might sanctify and cleanse it with the washing of water by the word, 27 and that He might present to Himself a glorious church, not having spot, or wrinkle, or any such thing, but that it should be holy and without blemish. 28 In this way men ought to love their wives as their own bodies. He who loves his wife loves himself

Your relationship should be spiritual in that you encourage each other to be the best possible. This would include praying for each other's gifts and talents and success as though you were praying for yourself. Normally the wife gets special intuition about things, and if she is a godly woman, she is praying about them and speaking to her husband about them.

Made One

The husband is to love God first and his wife next. The same is true of the wife. God must be first and her husband next. If they truly keep these as the priorities, their relationship will go smoothly. I knew of a pastor who would not let people get divorced until they met with her. She would get them both to come together and she moved mightily in the gift of prophecy and word of wisdom and word of knowledge. She would often pray with them, and before the end of the meeting they would both be repenting for their neglect or abuse of the other. They got right with God; they got right with each other. This would be the best way for our churches to function. Not all pastors have those same prophetic giftings,

I know of a couple who were married more than 30 years who loved each other and had a glow of joy about them. They loved each other and they both were servants in the church. They shared with me one of the best resolutions to arguments that I've ever known. They both agreed together they would never let the sun go down without making up with each other. What they would do, is get a basin of warm water and a towel and even if they were mad at each other, they would pray for the other person and wash the person's feet.

As you are kneeling there at your spouse's feet loving the person as Christ loved his disciples, as you pray blessings over the person and scriptures, God will empty you of any self-righteousness or pride. People who do this – put Christ first, no matter how they are feeling, are sure to stay together. They both agree that Christ is first. I would also recommend taking communion with your spouse and recommitting yourselves to each other with prayer. A man and woman who are in union with God are unstoppable. They can do much for Christ's kingdom together. They must be in agreement. You cannot yoke a donkey and an ox because both walk differently. They must both walk the same. Your point of agreement in your marriage should always be that God is the center.

Don't Eliminate Christ from your Marriage

Don't forget that God is the center of your personal life and your marriage. Don't let anything replace your conversations with your spouse. Television should never be the focus of the family. It is for entertainment; it should never take priority over your spouse. Don't let your cell phone be your priority. Don't put anything above your relationship with God or with your spouse. It doesn't mean the other things can't be a part of what you do but they should never define you.

The reason the Apostle Paul states that some people should remain single as himself is because the husband must care for his wife. The wife must care for her husband. It is a commandment that God gives. A married person can't do anything he or she wants without speaking to his or her spouse and discussing it. You become not only accountable to God but also to each other.

You and your spouse should be praying together every day. I understand that children and pets and working spouses etc. add some complexity but there should be moments of sincere prayer for each other each day.

I have known couples who have been married, 30, 40, 50 years or longer, who lived faithfully loving each other keeping God first. I have known others who lived through terrible things such as unfaithfulness of a spouse but they were reconciled and their marriage was restored. With God in your marriage, you will never lose. Should a couple shut God out of their marriage, most certainly they will not love each other with the unconditional love I have mentioned. They could end in divorce. There are excellent books on marriage by Myles Munroe. I highly recommend them. They give a Christ centered teaching on marriage and how to truly love your spouse.

Your inviting of God into the marriage ceremony is not only as a witness that one day you got married. It is for God to be the head of your marriage relationship all the days of your life. This is the sacrament aspect that is spiritual. God is dwelling in both of you and also in your covenant made to each other with God.

If you Wonder if You're Ready, you are not

Do not marry too quickly. The ideal is that you both would have done some Bible study together and talked about spiritual things as well as natural things. You would know the other person's likes and dislikes. You may know the other person's weaknesses and strengths. Examine all these things before you get married; don't marry so you can change the other person. You should be able to share with your potential spouse as with the closest friend the desires of your heart knowing that he or she will care and pray about them and want the best possible for you also. Just as God wants to give you the desires of your heart, your spouse should want you to be joyful and successful.

Psalm 37: 4 4 Delight yourself in the Lord,
   and He will give you the desires of your heart.

A Recommendation for Those who Want to Marry

Many people get married in the Romance stage of the marriage. This means the other person seems perfect and the attraction is so strong he or she doesn't notice the habits of the person or the person's demeanor or the person's mannerisms. Usually, I would recommend the couple wait at least a year. It is not stated as such in scripture; I only speak by personal experience and many people I have known who married and are successful and also some who are not. I also believe they should be doing spiritual studying together as well as prayer and serving, The more they use their spiritual giftings together, the smoother they will see how to complement each other. Get to know the person's behaviour before you marry.

1 Corinthians 7: 9 But if they cannot restrain themselves, let them marry. For it is better to marry than to burn with passion.

Adultery and Fornication

Exodus 20: 14 You shall not commit adultery.

The commandment is for singles as well as married people. There is to be no sex outside of marriage. The commandment is clear but in our society it is not honoured. There are even Christians who are engaged to be married who are tempted and have sexual relations outside of marriage: fornication. They may believe it is okay because they plan to marry eventually. It is sin. I heard of Kenneth Copeland talk about this matter and it was excellent. He said that you should both repent. Get with your fiancée and both of you confess it to God and plead the blood over yourselves and commit to God that from that moment on you will remain pure before marriage. Kenneth Copeland said to take communion with one another and vow to live holy so that God will bless you and bless your marriage. If we truly repent, God forgives us and empowers us so that we do not have to live in sin.

Spiritual Aspects of Marriage

The two people are joining their lives and they will likely have children.

Most people marry for that purpose; it is not the only reason to marry but Biblically, God did command them to be fruitful and multiply. God never revoked His word. Should you have children, you both need wisdom from God. To nurture and encourage the children as well as teach them spiritual and natural things, requires spiritual discernment and divine leading. Marriage is a most serious, solemn covenant that should not be considered lightly. If you commit adultery in your marriage, you are not only breaking your covenant with your spouse but also with God. Neglecting your spouse, or drawing apart from him or her is also a sin. Some people say they grew apart. That should be impossible because marriage is the two becoming one. That means there must be communion, a sharing of lives, not simply sexual relations. If you do not want to live together as one, you should not be getting married.

1 Corinthians 7: 5 Do not deprive one another except with consent for a time, that you may give yourselves to fasting and prayer. Then come together again, so that Satan does not tempt you for lack of self-control.

Marriage means a joining together until the death of the spouse except by mutual agreement. If you are not sure you are ready to join your life to someone, don't marry. God's standard for marriage is high; it is a lifelong commitment. You should consider the person you marry carefully. You should learn each other's character traits before you marry. Our churches should preach commitment for life marriage. God can give you special love for your spouse. God can correct your spouse. I don't know if you have seen the movie War Room that came out in 2016, but it was an excellent movie about prayer and how God can save a marriage if one of the partners is praying. I knew of a miraculous restoration of a marriage.

The man and woman were Christians. As their marriage became seasoned, he cheated (had relationships with other women) on her more and more. He ended the marriage relationship by leaving the woman and moving in with his girlfriend. He completely turned away from God as well as his spouse. They became divorced. It was not her decision but it happened. That woman was a prayer warrior. She prayed over her husband – she never broke her part of the covenant with God.

She was an attractive woman with money. She could have found a different person. She chose to pray for him. She would pray for him to repent and for the resurrection of her marriage based on God's covenant with the both of them. She did this day after day, year after year. She still loved him. He did not treat her well if they saw each other, it only bothered her more so she moved to a different state, but she continued the praying and would make visits home to see her family and hear about her ex-husband. For twenty years, she prayed and travailed and kept the prayer faithfully for his repentance and the resurrection of their marriage.

I do not know of anyone else who had the vision so clear for her marriage to be restored. Perhaps people might have thought she was extreme because she did not give up on him. One day, it happened. It came as a surprise to all of us who knew about her situation but not to her. She shouted and danced and praised God with all her being. He repented. He begged her to come back. He rededicated his life to God. They remarried. Twenty years of constant believing and praying, she saw the desire of her heart. She believed God would do it. God would never violate a human will. Even though he made terrible choices and abandoned her and turned away from God, God let him. She completely had grace to forgive him.

Divorced

There is mercy for people who have sinned. There is one acceptable reason for divorce and remarriage. It is not God's perfect plan but He allows it. If one of the person's is unfaithful, divorce is permitted. They can remarry freely.

Matthew 19: 8 He said to them, "Moses, for the hardness of your hearts, permitted you to divorce your wives, but from the beginning it was not so. 9 But I say to you, whoever divorces his wife, except for sexual immorality, and marries another, commits adultery. And whoever marries her who is divorced commits adultery."

There are a multitude of reasons for divorce. Abuse, neglect, character traits, habits etc. Please know that I know the divorce rate is high. There is mercy for those who sin. I'm saying with boldness God can forgive you for any sin. Go to Jesus; even if it is not your doing, pray submitting yourself wholly to God and giving yourself to God. I have known of people who God shines light on and their lives are resurrected. Divorce is so tough one people because first, it is a covenant with the partner and with God. Only God can heal someone who has suffered from divorce. The good news is that God can and does heal.

Christian Parents

A Christian mother should in all matters teach the children the things of God. Usually, but not always does the mother spend more time with the children than their dad does. She should read with them, pray with them as well as help them in all natural matters. So should he care for them. I have known of single moms and single dads who invest all their efforts into the raising of the children. I have seen these single parents training their children in the best way possible even though they are working, paying bills, speaking with an uncooperative spouse etc. It is really God's mercy over them. Christian parents are a covering for their children until their children are old enough to accept Jesus themselves.

Deuteronomy 11: 19 You shall teach them to your children, speaking of them when you sit in your house and when you walk by the way, when you lie down, and when you rise up.

Both the husband and the wife should have separate prayer as well as prayer together. I have known of Christian husbands who would arise and go to 6am prayer services before work. They knew God had entrusted his family to him. He knew that only with God could he get wisdom and discernment and knowledge to lead and cover in prayer as a shield of protection over his family. I have known of Christian women who would rise early to begin praying before the school day. They would pray evenings and throughout the day. I mean they would pray about their children and family members as well as others. They literally were living the apostle Paul's commandment to "Pray without ceasing." 1 Thessalonians 5: 17.

Christian Family Anointing

Christian marriage partners should be growing spiritually together as well as individually. This type of bonding usually comes through sharing Christian service such as evangelism or praise teams or serving together during church functions. I have been privileged to know a Christian family of worshippers. As they lead worship, they flowed together so smoothly and completely in the Holy Spirit. The family radiated the love of God as they worshipped. It was a special family anointing on them as they worshipped together. They all have individual talents and ministry giftings but as a family, a unique dynamic occurs as the Holy Spirit fills them and flows through them.

I believe every Christian couple has a ministry anointing. I believe that every Christian family has an anointing for service. They should pray and seek God about what they are to do as a family. I believe God will speak to both the husband and the wife. I believe that God will confirm the word. The family will find joy in serving the LORD together. I have seen families volunteer to serve at banquets or who cook together, or who minister together, preaching and teaching God. I believe that the Husband and the wife should pray for a vision of what God would have them to do as a family. It is a spiritual union with God in the midst of it. God wants to use you as a family to impact the earth for God.

6 DEDICATION OF CHILDREN

The Dedication of Children – Sacrament

In most Protestant Churches, this sacrament is practiced. In some denominations, the children are Christened – meaning they are baptized but not immersed in the water – sprinkled with water. It is really a way of the parents agreeing to raise their children as Christians. The Bible teaches believer's baptism, that is total immersion over someone proclaiming to believe that Jesus Christ died for all sinners, rose from the dead and ascended into heaven and is coming again. Children who are infants who do not know the LORD Jesus Christ as their personal Saviour and LORD should be dedicated by the parents. It is a way of honouring the LORD. It is a way of presenting the child to God, in agreement with the Word of God that instructs parents to teach their children the Word of God. It means the parents are living as Christians and will instruct their children in the ways of God.

Usually, dedication of children is scheduled as part of the church service. The parents dress the children in the cutest outfits and they stand with the pastor and sometimes the elders who will pray blessings over the child. A scripture may be read or prayed over the child. The parents are standing before the congregation to pledge they will raise their children as Christians. The congregation is praying that the child will come to know Christ at an early age. The pastor usually consecrates the child by praying that God would bless and keep the child.

In some churches, prayer is made that the parents will be faithful in the raising of their children to serve God. Although prayer for the parents is good, the dedication of children should be about praying over the children. The fact that the parents are coming in front of the church with their child or children, is usually a testimony of them wanting to raise the child as a Christian.

At some baby dedications, there is prophesy over the children. Usually it is the pastor or the ministry team who pray prophetically over the children, as the Holy Spirit leads. What that means is, the Holy Spirit is the author of the prophecy. God gives the person the unction, the words and the anointing to pray prophetically over the children.

Not a Ritual

We do not simply carry our children in front of the church so that people can see them and how cute they are. It is not simply an outward action. If there is no faith, there is nothing that happens. The parents must believe that dedicating their children is a consecration of the children and the hope for a blessing to be imparted by the prayers of the ministers and the local body of Christ. I'm saying we believe the children are separated unto God and "covered" by the faith of the parents.

1 Corinthians 7: 14 For the unbelieving husband is sanctified by the wife, and the unbelieving wife is sanctified by the husband. Otherwise, your children would be unclean. But now they are holy.

Sacrament

There are two parts because it is a sacrament. There is a natural presentation of the children in front of the pastors and congregation and there is a spiritual proclamation of consecration of the children to God. It is a way of honouring what Jesus did by laying hands on children and praying a blessing over them.

Matthew 19: 13 Then little children were brought to Him that He might put His hands on them and pray. But the disciples rebuked them.

14 But Jesus said, "Let the little children come to Me, and do not forbid them. For to such belongs the kingdom of heaven." 15 He laid His hands on them and departed from there.

Jesus Shows Priorities

Jesus corrected his disciples who perhaps believed the children were not important. Jesus called for the children and prayed blessings over them. I do not believe Jesus was doing a ritual. I am sure Jesus was truly imparting a blessing. It was Jesus, the Messiah, God himself in human form. He was praying blessings on the children. He was praying the best possible life for those children. Jesus wants the best for us. If He believed it was important to bless the children, we also should see the significance.

Luke 18: 15 They also brought infants to Him that He might touch them. When the disciples saw it, they rebuked them. 16 But Jesus called them to Him and said, "Permit the little children to come to Me, and do not hinder them. For to such belongs the kingdom of God. 17 Truly, I say to you, whoever will not receive the kingdom of God as a little child will in no wise enter it."

Jesus used the children to preach to the people. He preached that all must receive the kingdom of God as innocently and with pure motives as children would press into someone they loved. It is normal for a child or children to cling to their parents especially in a new environment. We also should press into Jesus. We should know He wants only the best for us as a parent would shelter a child.

Jesus' Dedication as a Child

Luke 2: 21 When eight days had passed and the Child was circumcised, He was named JESUS, the name given by the angel before He was conceived in the womb.

22 When the days of her purification according to the Law of Moses were completed, they brought Him to Jerusalem to present Him to the Lord 23 (as it is written in the law of the Lord, "Every firstborn male shall be called holy to the Lord"[a]) 24 and to offer a sacrifice according to what is said in the law of the Lord, "a pair of turtledoves, or two young pigeons."[b]

Prophetic Prayer

Jesus himself was presented for circumcision and to offer a sacrifice thanking God for the child. Mary and Joseph honoured the LORD in obeying the Mosaic covenant. Simeon a prophet of God who prayed constantly that he could live to see the Messiah that would come to redeem Israel was present in the temple and was moved by the Holy Spirit to prophesy over Jesus.

Luke 2: 29 "Lord, now let Your servant depart in peace,
     according to Your word;
30 for my eyes have seen Your salvation
31   which You have prepared in the sight of all people,
32 a light for revelation to the Gentiles,   and the glory of Your people Israel."

Simeon also prophesied over Mary. He gave words that she would hold on to throughout the life and death of Jesus.

Luke 2: Listen, this Child is destined to cause the fall and rising of many in Israel and to be a sign which will be spoken against, 35 so that the thoughts of many hearts may be revealed. And a sword will pierce through your own soul also."

Also, in the temple praying was Anna, a godly woman who gave her life to prayer and fasting after her husband died. She also was moved by the Holy Spirit to prophesy over the infant Jesus.

Luke 2: 36 And there was Anna a prophetess, a daughter of Phanuel, of the tribe of Asher. She was of a great age and had lived with her husband seven years from her virginity. 37 And she was a widow of about eighty-four years of age who did not depart from the temple, but served God with fasting and prayer night and day. 38 Coming at that moment she gave thanks to the Lord and spoke of Him to all those who looked for the redemption of Jerusalem.

The Prophesying is Important

The prophecies over the children are important. It was important for Jesus. Those two individuals did not know the miraculous birth of Jesus or his destiny except through the Holy Spirit. Any special prayers or prophesy over the children should be recorded so that they could be used for prayer and for guidance for the parents and those who raise the child. Some prophesies may come over a child. It may or may not occur depending on may factors. Some ministers do not flow in the prophetic so they wouldn't be moved to prophesy. Some churches are on strict schedules so they may not wait for the promptings of the Spirit for the prophetic. It doesn't necessarily automatically come for each child. If there were a gathering of Apostles and prophets praying over the children, I would expect there to be prophesy over the children. Not everyone flows in these giftings or in these expectations from the LORD.

The Dedication of the Child

The dedication of a child is an announcement in the faith of God for their child or children to become Christians. They are literally giving the best offering they could give to God – that child or those children. The parents are promising to obey God. The minister consecrates the child. The congregation prays for the child.

The Mosaic Covenant

According to the Mosaic covenant, all of the first born of all creatures were to be given to God. The first-born animals, were given as a sacrifice.

The children were redeemed by giving an offering. It was a way of remembering the miracles God did to set Israel free from Egyptian bondage – especially the Passover celebration. It was a way of thanking God and giving the best offering possible to thank God for the child.

Exodus 22: 29 You must not delay to offer the first of your harvest and of your vats.

You must give to Me the firstborn of your sons. 30 Likewise you must do the same with your oxen and with your sheep. Seven days it shall remain with its mother, but on the eighth day you must give it to Me.

Exodus 13:
13 But every first offspring of a donkey you shall redeem with a lamb. And if you do not redeem it, then you shall break its neck, and all the firstborn of man among your sons you shall redeem.

14 "It shall be when your son asks you in time to come, saying, 'What is this?' that you shall say to him, 'With a strong hand the Lord brought us out from Egypt, from the house of bondage. 15 And when Pharaoh stubbornly refused to let us go, that the Lord killed all the firstborn in the land of Egypt, both the firstborn of man, and the firstborn of beast. Therefore, I sacrifice to the Lord the first male offspring of every womb, but all the firstborn of my sons I redeem.' 16 It shall be as a sign on your hand and as frontlets on your forehead, for with a strong hand the Lord brought us out of Egypt."

Hanna prays for a child

Hanna in the Old testament book of Samuel wanted a child so much she prayed and fasted in the temple until one day the priest blessed her by saying may the Lord grant you your request. She made a vow to God that if God would open her womb so that she may have a child, she would give him to God for service. Within a year of that priest's words of blessing and much praying by Hanna, she gave birth to a son and named him Samuel.

1 Samuel 1: 21 Then the man Elkanah and all his house went up to offer to the Lord the yearly sacrifice and his vow. 22 But Hannah did not go, for she said to her husband, "I will not go up until the child is weaned, and then I will bring him, that he may appear before the Lord and live there forever."

She cared for the child and after he was weaned, she presented him at the Temple to the priest as she had promised God she would do. She brought Samuel and an offering to God thanking God for the child and to consecrate the child to the service of God. She presented the best that she had to God – the child she had prayed for. The child Samuel was raised by the priest. He was trained to serve the LORD. Each year Hanna brought clothing for her son. God blessed her with other children because she kept her vow. A vow to God is very important.

1 Samuel 1: 24 When she had weaned him, she took him up with her with three bulls, one ephah[b] of flour, and a bottle of wine. And she brought him to the house of the Lord in Shiloh, though the boy was young. 25 Then they slaughtered a bull, and they brought the boy to Eli. 26 And she said, "Oh, my lord! As you live, my lord, I am the woman that stood by you here praying to the Lord. 27 For this boy I prayed, and the Lord has given me my petition which I asked of Him. 28 Therefore also I have let the Lord have him. As long as he lives he will be dedicated to the Lord." And he worshipped the Lord there.

Children are a gift from God

One of the main commandments God gave to Adam and Eve and later Noah is to have as many children as possible. God commanded that they be fruitful and multiply. Children were treasured by their parents. Not only would they help with the family business once they were older, they would carry on the family name. They would pass on the truths they had learned about God to their children. Through this there would be a godly people on earth who worshipped Jehovah.

Psalm 127: 3 Look, children are a gift of the Lord,
   and the fruit of the womb is a reward.
4 As arrows in the hand of a mighty warrior,
   so are the children of one's youth.
5 Happy is the man
   who has his quiver full of them;
he shall not be ashamed
   when he speaks with the enemies at the gate.

Children are precious and we can teach our children to love, honour and live for God. It should come from the parents, the church and the school agreeing together in raising the children to become Christians. God intrusts to us a living soul. God gives us special responsibility and special joys in seeing the kids raised to honour God. Parents, teachers and people in the lives of children should nurture the gifts and talents in the children. We should teach them and encourage them in all spiritual truths as well as in their natural abilities.

Proverbs 22: 6 Train up a child in the way he should go,
   and when he is old he will not depart from it.

The parents who treasure their children and that serve God wholly will be gifted by God to have good relationship with their children and also be able to see the "way" for each child. This means each child is an individual and has special gifts and talents to be nurtured and encouraged. Teachers who love their students will be able to see the special expressions of talent in each child. Together parents, teachers and the local church members can contribute to the children by giving them the best possible care.

The Potential of a Child

God may entrust to our care one who will become a world evangelist, or a professor or an inventor or a doctor. Each child encouraged in his or her talents can explore gifts and talents and develop them so they are used for God's glory. A child is a gift from God. The child has some of the characteristics of each parent. The child is also unique. I have not met a Christian parent who does not believe the child is a gift from God. As the child grows, individual traits and giftings become more prominent and the child's character is formed and his or her interests can be encouraged. For example, the children can take music lessons so they can play an instrument; they can be taught to play sports. They can be taught in the word of God so that they can accept the LORD as children. All of these things can be developed before the children go to school.

It is the pleasure of the parent to see the giftings in the child. Teachers also can encourage the children to do their best. Often, I can see the child's particular giftings by teaching him or her and speaking with him or her individually. Parents should invest in their children. The child can learn and develop all types of talents including music, sports, reading, writing, math, science, etc. The things a child "leans towards" or enjoys will become evident in their early years. It is the responsibility of parents to help their children become the best possible people they can be. I have known of parents who sacrifice much for their children. They drive them to sporting events; music lessons; concerts; children's programs and events. They buy them books; they care for their children because their children are an expression of God's love to them. They realize God has given them a tremendous responsibility as well as a joy like no other.

Parenting

Christian parents are obligated to God as they promise to raise their children. Children who do not have parents that invest in them can raise themselves but it is not good. If the television is the main teacher of the child, the child will not learn God's ways. If a child is not encouraged in his or her talents and skills, those talents and skills go untapped and undeveloped. The children will do other things – it will depend on who does invest in the children.

For instance, a child left to himself or herself will hang out with children in the neighbourhood. That could be good or bad, depending on what those children are like. A loving neighbour can teach the children. He or she can share Christ with them. He or she can encourage and mentor them. A Sunday school teacher can care about the children. A teacher from school can make a difference. The main chunk will be missing though and that is what the parents should be doing.

Deuteronomy 11: 18 Therefore you must fix these words of mine in your heart and in your soul, and bind them as a sign on your hand, so that they may be as frontlets between your eyes. 19 You shall teach them to your children, speaking of them when you sit in your house and when you walk by the way, when you lie down, and when you rise up. 20 You shall write them on the doorposts of your house and on your gates, 21 so that your days and the days of your children may be multiplied in the land which the Lord swore to your fathers to give them, as long as the days of heaven on the earth.

The bottom line is if the parents won't raise the children, someone will, but the parents will be accountable for not doing their best with what God has entrusted to them. The responsibility of parents is to teach their children the ways of the LORD, to provide food and shelter and love. The parents should be helping the children with their homework, take interest in their schooling and their lessons. The parents should encourage the children's dreams and aspirations and be prayerful about all aspects of parenting. If the children are living in your home, they are within the sphere of your authority.

The Parents who Dedicate their Children

The parents who dedicate their children are coming into agreement with God concerning the raising of the child. The parents are agreeing to do the best possible to train up their children.

Hands should be laid on the child to pray, to confirm gifts and talents and to completely agree on raising that child for God's best possible life.

At the church, I currently attend, the parents choose a scripture to pray over their child at dedication. I would highly encourage that those scriptures be prayerfully chosen. If the parents will join their faith to the scriptures they pray over their children, God will honour their faith.

God can give special wisdom and knowledge to Christian parents who will go with the promptings of the Holy Spirit for their children. If the parents are living in the Spirit, God will deal with them in the Spirit. If they seriously, prayerfully raise their children, God will give special insight and wisdom. God will hold us accountable for our dealings with our children because there is a spiritual responsibility that we have to model a Christian life for them and to train them up as Christians.

By the Holy Spirit

The ministers and elders should be praying a spiritual blessing over the child but also that every gift and talent will be developed, that God would draw them so that an early age the child will give his or her life to God. God can use a minister of God who will obey the promptings of the LORD to prophesy a blessing over the child. It is not simply an outward ritual. It is a faith expression and an offering to commit to raise the children to the best of their ability: the parents, the church agreeing.

As Hanna gave her son Samuel to be raised by the priest Eli, she kept her vow, so should the parents offer their children to God to be raised as unto God. As you are standing on the platform about to dedicate your child or children, God may speak to you concerning the child's life. Parents who will rely on the Holy Spirit will be guided by God in the raising of their children. God may use you in special ways to pray over your children or give you scriptures concerning your children. You should pray over your children everyday thanking God for them and praying protection and encouragement. Parenting by the Holy Spirit is God's best for your children. God can give you words of wisdom or knowledge about your children.

Sins can be passed from generation to generation. Don't let them Be. Cut them off with your generation. God can give you discerning of spirits to know if your child has inherited iniquities that must be cut off. Inherited sins can end with you as you pray over yourself and your children. If you see any type of repetitive sin in your child, you should seek God about it and deal with it in the spirit first. Cut those things off in prayer.

Numbers 14: 17 "So now, I pray, let the power of my Lord be great, just as You have spoken, saying, 18 'The Lord is slow to anger and abounding in mercy, forgiving iniquity and transgression; but He will by no means clear the guilty, visiting the iniquity of the fathers upon the children to the third and fourth generation.' 19 Pardon the iniquity of this people, I pray, according to the greatness of Your grace, just as You have pardoned this people, from Egypt even until now."

Pray in the Spirit for your children. I attended a church where we were often in long prayer meetings. You might think that the young parents wouldn't go. No. This was not the case. Parents would bring their children and a blanket. They would set their children in a place with toys or their infant in a carrier and they would attend to them – but they didn't miss prayer because of it. Their children were in an atmosphere of praise and worship and prayer often for hours. I'm not saying that the parents didn't go check on their children regularly. The fact is the children were in a atmosphere of the Holy Spirit so strong that as soon they were able to walk, they would go up to the altar and start singing and praising God themselves. No one told them to do it. The children of all ages (and adults) would sing and dance and praise God with all their being.

Search the Scriptures

Pray scriptures over your children. Most Christian bookstores carry books on the promises of God. Get a book on praying the scriptures for your children. There are books that you could get on imparting a blessing over your children. Marilyn Hickey has got an excellent book on imparting a legacy to the next generation. Pray over your children those scriptures. God may reveal something to you about the direction of your child's life. God may reveal to you to pray special protection over your child. I don't only mean while they are children. I have known of parents who pray over their children all the days of their lives. Their children are adults with children of their own, but the parents pray special blessings on their adult children. The calling to be a parent doesn't end once the child leaves home. The calling to be a parent is for all your life. long.

Please understand, I am not talking about being burdensome or smothering. Once your children marry or move out of your home, you don't have the same responsibility towards them in the natural; spiritually though, you should be praying for them. I am saying the responsibility to give your children to God only ends once your natural life ends on earth.

Often the grandparents can be a strong influence. You can contribute not only to your own children's lives but also to their children's lives. This means grandparents who are being led by the Holy Spirit can make a difference in their grandchildren's lives. I know of some grandparents who were the only Christians, the parents were not living for God; those grandparents taught their grandchildren all they could about God. They invested in them scriptures, Bible stories, Sunday school etc.

Serious Prayer

I have known of Christian parents who pray for their children before the children go to school each day. Each evening, they pray a blessing over them as they tuck them in. The parents talk about God with their children and it is a normal part of their life to talk about God. The parents monitor what the children watch or listen to. The child is never left alone with only the television; these parents watch television with their children or approve of what the child sees or hears. These parents are a literal spiritual covering over the children protecting them from worldly or ungodly content.

Please, if you are a single parent, do not be insulted by any of my teaching. I understand single parents cannot invest as much as they want to into their children. I've known single moms who work two jobs to raise her children. It is tough on that parent. That is where the Christian Church should help. Offering child care in the services is very important because it gives a chance for those single parents to receive something of God. It also gives special Christian education to the children. I have been a part of some churches where the single young adults voluntarily "adopt" a child. What I mean is they will take the child to concerts or shows, play sports with the children and offer a relief to the single parent as well as a support role in the life of the child/children.

In my church, we do not have godparents. Often the term is used and any special friend is chosen. The true meaning of godparents is that if anything were to happen to the child's parents, those people would give the best possible care to the child, teaching them about the LORD. I believe it would be a wise thing to develop in all our Christian churches spiritual God Parents who would help especially single parents to raise their children as Christians. Not just anyone should be chosen. The person should be of outstanding Christian character and faith. The people should serve and honour the LORD and love you and your child. Only God can put people together in the way I am speaking about. They could be aunts and uncles or true friends. God could direct you in it. I know of no congregation such as what I am presenting, so I believe it would be up to you to seek God for wisdom about such a proposition. I believe it is essential for a child to have godly role models both men and women.

Child dedication is not always recognized in importance as it should be. God will honour you at your point of faith. Believe that God can use you to be a spiritual influence on your child. You are honouring God by presenting your child in dedication to God. You are making a covenant with God promising to raise the child and offering him or her unto God.

7 ANOINTING WITH OIL AND HEALING

Sacrament of Anointing with Oil

Anointing with oil is symbolic of joy and prosperity and blessing of God. Part of the promise to Israel is that God would bring them to a fertile land of milk and honey. That means there would be trees and flowers and vegetables. Israel is famous for Olive trees and excellent olive oil. Oil represented wealth, prosperity, peace, joy, similar to how we in North America view the horn of plenty at Thanksgiving.

The first instruction to anoint with oil is given to Moses to anoint Aaron and his sons to be high priests for Israel. The oil is symbolic of the Holy Spirit and sanctifying or setting apart of something, whether people, animals, or objects for the service of God.

Exodus 29: 7 Take the anointing oil and anoint him by pouring it on his head.

Oil Instructed by God

God gave special instructions for Moses to create a Holy oil – that is that it was only to be used by the Levites and it could not be used for personal pleasure such as perfume. It was a sanctifying oil but God gave the recipe. The spices mentioned would have given it a sweet smell. The priests were to sanctify all the objects used for worship with this anointing oil. It was completely forbidden for them to use the oil for their own purposes. It was completely forbidden for others to make the oil. It was only meant for the priests and they were given strict instructions on how to use it. Whatever the priests anointed with oil was to be set apart for the priests to use in worship to God.

Exodus 30: 22 Then the Lord said to Moses, 23 "Take the following fine spices: 500 shekels[d] of liquid myrrh, half as much (that is, 250 shekels) of fragrant cinnamon, 250 shekels[e] of fragrant calamus, 24 500 shekels of cassia—all according to the sanctuary shekel—and a hin[f] of olive oil. 25 Make these into a sacred anointing oil, a fragrant blend, the work of a perfumer. It will be the sacred anointing oil. 26 Then use it to anoint the tent of meeting, the ark of the covenant law, 27 the table and all its articles, the lampstand and its accessories, the altar of incense, 28 the altar of burnt offering and all its utensils, and the basin with its stand. 29 You shall consecrate them so they will be most holy, and whatever touches them will be holy.

Leviticus 8: 2 "Bring Aaron and his sons, their garments, the anointing oil, the bull for the sin offering,[a]

Saul Anointed as King

The prophet Samuel was instructed by God to take a flask of oil and anoint Saul as the first king of Israel. This was a symbol of the Holy Spirit and anointing from God or God's approval of the person as ruler.

1 Samuel 10: 1 Then Samuel took a flask of olive oil and poured it on Saul's head and kissed him, saying, "Has not the Lord anointed you ruler over his inheritance?[a] 2 When you leave me today, you will meet two men near Rachel's tomb, at Zelzah on the border of Benjamin.
David anointed as King

After Saul sinned against of the LORD and did not repent, David was anointed as king of Israel while he was still a youth. Samuel was instructed by God to go to Jesse's and anoint one of his sons as the next king of Israel. As Samuel discerned the boys standing in front of them none of them was chosen by God, until David came in later. God spoke to Samuel.

1 Samuel 16: Then the Lord said, "Rise and anoint him; this is the one."

13 So Samuel took the horn of oil and anointed him in the presence of his brothers, and from that day on the Spirit of the Lord came powerfully upon David. Samuel then went to Ramah.

Even though the horn of oil (a Ram's horn was used) was poured on David, he was not king for many more years. It was of special significance because God sent the prophet Samuel to do it showing it was God's choice. Also, it significantly set apart David by God to become King. That meant his life that followed lead to kingship. It was an outward sign of God's choice and God's blessing. It was special to those who witnessed it and was special to David because he could not forget such an event.

Throughout the Old Testament oil is used as a symbol of prosperity and joy for God's people.

Psalm 104: 14 He makes grass grow for the cattle,
and plants for people to cultivate—

bringing forth food from the earth:
15 wine that gladdens human hearts,
   oil to make their faces shine,
   and bread that sustains their hearts

The Sacrament of Anointing with oil

Anointing with oil

   In charismatic, full gospel or Pentecostal churches oil is used to pray for people. I have not ever seen oil poured on a person as it was in the old testament. I have both received and administered the sacrament of anointing with oil. It is to be considered seriously. If there is a person who is ill, that person should get the elders to pray for him or her believing for healing. It is not expected that God's people should be ill. God's will is clearly healing for His people. The oil is not considered to be holy. It is faith that is the key aspect of this type of prayer.

   The first condition is that if the person is too ill to go to church, he or she should contact the elders of the church to come pray for him or her. Calling the elders to come pray is an act of faith. You wouldn't call them if you didn't believe that God was going to keep His word. Next the elders are to be praying over the person anointing him or her with oil. The oil represents the Holy Spirit and the anointing of the oil is a contact point for the faith of both the recipient and the elders. God's word promises that if they will pray for the sick, they will be healed. It is the prayer of faith that is to be prayed over the person. The prayer of faith means you pray believing that God's word teaches healing. There can also be healing and forgiveness for sins as this prayer is administered.

James 5: 13 Is anyone among you in trouble? Let them pray. Is anyone happy? Let them sing songs of praise. 14 Is anyone among you sick? Let them call the elders of the church to pray over them and anoint them with oil in the name of the Lord. 15 And the prayer offered in faith will make the sick person well; the Lord will raise them up. If they have sinned, they will be forgiven. 16 Therefore confess your sins to each other and pray for each other so that you may be healed. The prayer of a righteous person is powerful and effective.

Inner Healing

   Jesus Christ died for our sins but also died so we could be healed and delivered also. Please see that Jesus died for our sins and iniquities so that we might be saved. Also true though, is that he took stripes on his back and endured beatings so that by his wounds we could be healed. It is not only symbolic spiritual healing that is being talked about here but deep healing of the person's soul and also of the body. If a person will believe the words of scripture and hold to them, God can bring healing in the deepest parts of a person's life. It is not some type of willful personal strength. It is faith in God's word that releases a miracle for the person. The Messiah bore all our griefs and sorrows.

Isaiah 53: 4 Surely he took up our pain
    and bore our suffering,
yet we considered him punished by God,
    stricken by him, and afflicted.
5 But he was pierced for our transgressions,
    he was crushed for our iniquities;
the punishment that brought us peace was on him,
    and by his wounds we are healed.
6 We all, like sheep, have gone astray,
    each of us has turned to our own way;
and the Lord has laid on him
    the iniquity of us all.

Jesus Died to Give you Peace

The words "the punishment that brought us peace" means he suffered and died so that we might peace. People who are deeply wounded by person tragedies such as divorce or the death of a loved one can believe the word of God that Jesus came to bring us peace that passes all understanding.

Also, God's Word promises us deliverance. That means a person can be set free from addictions or any type of habitual sin. This is further described in a different Messianic prophesy.

Isaiah 61: The Spirit of the Sovereign Lord is on me,
    because the Lord has anointed me
    to proclaim good news to the poor.
He has sent me to bind up the brokenhearted,
    to proclaim freedom for the captives
    and release from darkness for the prisoners,[a]
2 to proclaim the year of the Lord's favor
    and the day of vengeance of our God,
to comfort all who mourn,

3   and provide for those who grieve in Zion—
to bestow on them a crown of beauty
    instead of ashes,
the oil of joy
    instead of mourning,
and a garment of praise
    instead of a spirit of despair.

Inner Healing

" He has sent me to bind up the brokenhearted,

There can be administering of healing of the broken hearted – healing by anointing him or her with oil and praying in faith the scriptures believing that Jesus heals the innermost person. The proclamation of freedom to the captives can only come through a believer who knows that God can do it.

Freedom to the Captives

"to proclaim freedom for the captives
    and release from darkness for the prisoners,[a]"

The prayer of faith over a contrite or repentant person can bring freedom from sin and addictions. You cannot pray deliverance for a person unless you know that God delivers. A doubting person should not be anointing people with oil praying the prayer of faith with them. The prayer of faith requires that there is faith in God's desire to make people whole. If there is no faith, there should not be an outward action of the sacrament – that would just be religious having no spiritual significance and of being good to no one. Their sins can be forgiven and they can be made whole. There should be no part of the person that is wounded or broken. God heals spirit, soul and body.

Forgiveness

It may be possible that a person who is ill can be harbouring bitterness or unforgiveness. It is wise to speak with the person first and ask if there is any unforgiveness towards any person or people. We are commanded to forgive. That means we have no ill will towards the person or persons. It means we completely give it to God knowing that God will handle it. Releasing it to God is the first step. The next part is to say out loud " I forgive so and so.." Even if you do not feel as though you forgive the person, you confess that you do. Why? Because God commanded it that's why. If you can, pray a blessing over the person. It is hard but do it anyway. Why? If people have unjustly used you, abused you, or sinned against you, God will fight against them. What that means is their sins against you could have eternal consequences for them if they don't repent. Pray mercy over them. Pray that God would bring revelation to them so they could repent. In no way does it condone their sins against you. In no way does it make you a weaker person. What it does is free you from the sin of bitterness and hatred. Attitude matters to God.

Matthew 6: 15 But if you do not forgive others their sins, your Father will not forgive your sins.

Matthew 18: 21 Then Peter came to Jesus and asked, "Lord, how many times shall I forgive my brother or sister who sins against me? Up to seven times?"

22 Jesus answered, "I tell you, not seven times, but seventy-seven times.[g]

23 "Therefore, the kingdom of heaven is like a king who wanted to settle accounts with his servants. 24 As he began the settlement, a man who owed him ten thousand bags of gold[h] was brought to him. 25 Since he was not able to pay, the master ordered that he and his wife and his children and all that he had be sold to repay the debt.

26 "At this the servant fell on his knees before him. 'Be patient with me,' he begged, 'and I will pay back everything.' 27 The servant's master took pity on him, canceled the debt and let him go.

28 "But when that servant went out, he found one of his fellow servants who owed him a hundred silver coins.[i] He grabbed him and began to choke him. 'Pay back what you owe me!' he demanded.

29 "His fellow servant fell to his knees and begged him, 'Be patient with me, and I will pay it back.'

30 "But he refused. Instead, he went off and had the man thrown into prison until he could pay the debt. 31 When the other servants saw what had happened, they were outraged and went and told their master everything that had happened.

32 "Then the master called the servant in. 'You wicked servant,' he said, 'I canceled all that debt of yours because you begged me to. 33 Shouldn't you have had mercy on your fellow servant just as I had on you?' 34 In anger

his master handed him over to the jailers to be tortured, until he should pay back all he owed.

35 "This is how my heavenly Father will treat each of you unless you forgive your brother or sister from your heart."

I need forgiveness from God all my life long throughout eternity. I must forgive. It is mandatory. Forgiveness holds the person who harbours it in a state like hell. The person keeps thinking of the negative thing and grows more bitter with each remembrance. God strictly warns us about this

Hebrews 12: 14 Make every effort to live in peace with everyone and to be holy; without holiness no one will see the Lord. 15 See to it that no one falls short of the grace of God and that no bitter root grows up to cause trouble and defile many.

A root of bitterness, can be watered and grow into a tree of hatred. It can affect your prayer life, your relationship with God, your relationship with people, and your physical body. The only hope for that person is to repent, turn towards God and forgive. As that person forgives, he or she will be healed in spirit, soul and body.

Anointed Cloths

Acts 19: 11 God did extraordinary miracles through Paul, 12 so that even handkerchiefs and aprons that had touched him were taken to the sick, and their illnesses were cured and the evil spirits left them.

This passage of scripture talks about the anointing for healing being evident by impartation into the cloth itself. Literally as a person is anointed to pray for healing, spiritual substance is imparted to a person or in this instance into material.

In most full gospel churches, four square churches, charismatic or Pentecostal churches, there is the practice of praying over cloths, usually with oil imparting faith for healing and praying the person who receives it will be healed. It is not just an outward symbol. It is not just a symbolic thing. Spiritual substance is imparted into the cloths.

I myself have received such cloths for myself and for my mother. The faith is not in the cloth. No; no. The faith is in the God who used the minister or elder to pray faith for healing into the cloth.

The sacrament of anointing of oil should be considered seriously by the person. The person should examine his or her own heart first. The person should go forward for prayer in church or if unable to go to church, call for the elders to come pray with him or her. I have known a multitude of people who have both administered this sacrament and received it to their own lives with complete and total healing.

The sacrament of Anointing with oil can bring an impartation of life, health, wholeness.

The person who receives the sacrament must do it:

By faith
Believe that it affecting him or her.
Receive the healing from Jesus.

Often, this simple but mighty sacrament is not considered in the priority it should be.

8 LAYING ON OF HANDS AND CONFIRMATION

Laying on of Hands

Hebrews 6: 1 Therefore, leaving the elementary principles of the doctrine of Christ, let us go on to maturity, not laying again a foundation of repentance from dead works and of faith toward God, 2 of instruction about washings, the laying on of hands, the resurrection of the dead, and eternal judgment.

In the foundation stones of the Christian faith, laying on of hands is named as an essential foundation. It is also a sacrament. Although it is often practiced in the Christian Church in most denominations, it is not always done with faith which means it is just an external action rather than a two-part sacrament. Whatever is not of faith cannot be considered sacred. It is impossible to please God without Faith.

The Laying on of Hands

The literal Biblical interpretation is that we Christians believe that as we place hands on someone and pray for him or her, a spiritual transaction occurs. There is a transference from spirit to spirit because of the Holy Spirit and the Holy faith to do so. The Holy Spirit anointing on a person can be transferred to a believer by placing hands on the person and prayer. Faith is imparted. Sometimes, healing is imparted; sometimes confirmation of truths learned is imparted. This does not mean that prayer without laying on of hands is not effective. Jesus laid hands on people and they were healed. In some situations, in scripture, the apostles laid their hands on people for any of the above reasons.

As the disciples preached Jesus Christ after Pentecost, they had boldness to preach the infilling of the Holy Spirit or the Baptism of the Holy Spirit. Sometimes, they simply prayed for the Spirit to come on a person, but in this instance as they shared about the Baptism of the Holy Spirit, they literally placed their hands on the believers in faith for the gift of the Holy Spirit to be given to these Samaritans.

In Acts 8: 17 Then they laid their hands on them, and they received the Holy Spirit.

Often a common method that God uses to baptism someone in the Holy Spirit is that believers filled with the Holy Spirit lay hands in faith to those who want the gift. I mean a literal transference such as this example. I throw a ball to you and you catch it in your hands. Substance is transferred. The Holy Spirit within us anoints us to lay hands for a spiritual purpose; there is a transference of spirit to spirit. The effects may not be immediate or they may be. Usually, what occurs with baptism of the Holy Spirit is that a person begins to glorify God and as he or she does, tongues the person has never learned come up out of the innermost being of the person. It is an impartation of the Holy Spirit. Jesus Christ Himself is the Baptizer and uses a Spirit filled willing vessel to flow through the vessel to a person such as copper wiring is used as a conduit for the flow of current.

Also, spiritual gifts can be imparted by the laying on of hands. An example of this is Where Moses lays hands on Joshua according to the commandment of God.

Numbers 27: 18 The Lord said to Moses, "Take Joshua the son of Nun, a man in whom is the Spirit, and lay your hand on him, 19 and cause him to stand before Eleazar the priest and before all the assembly, and command in their sight. 20 You will put some of your majesty on him, in order that all the assembly of the children of Israel will listen. 21 He will stand before Eleazar the priest, who will ask for him about the judgment of the Urim before the Lord. At his word will they go out, and at his word they will come in, both he and all the children of Israel with him, even all the assembly."

It is God who instructs Moses on what to do. God explains the transference of spirit to spirit. God promises to impart some of the anointing of Moses onto Joshua. Moses prays for Joshua to have wisdom and strength to lead Israel. It is done publicly with the approval of the priests. It is not only a transference but it shows the people of Israel what God is doing. God clearly chooses the successor to Moses. Moses did not decide by himself. The people see the results of obedience to God. What it does is build their faith and trust in Joshua. The results are that all of Joshua`s life, the people of Israel followed God and obeyed Joshua as a leader of the people.

They keep their promise to follow Joshua as they had followed Moses.

Joshua 1: 16 They answered Joshua, "All that you command us we will do, and wherever you send us we will go. 17 Just as we obeyed Moses in all things, we will obey you. May the Lord your God be with you, as He was with Moses! 18 Whoever rebels against your command and disobeys your words, in all that you command him, shall be put to death. Only be strong and courageous."

Joshua was not a stranger to the children of Israel. Joshua was close to Moses and was entrusted to help Moses. Joshua was mentored by Moses. The people of Israel knew him well. Moses, passes on gifts through the transference of spirit to spirit. The Bible says that a spirit of wisdom rested on Joshua because of it.

Barnabus and Saul

In this next instance the disciples were praying and someone prophesied that Barnabus and Saul should be separated unto God for ministry.

Acts 13: 2 As they worshipped the Lord and fasted, the Holy Spirit said, "Set apart for Me Barnabas and Saul for the work to which I have called them." 3 Then after fasting and praying, they laid their hands on them and sent them off.

Clearly it is not symbolic. The disciples prayed and fasted and laid hands and prayed. They seriously considered the action as sacred or holy. It is not simply a rite or an outward sign. It has significance. It is not a ritual. It is an expression of faith and an action done in faith so that God may use humans as vessels that He can pour His glory through.

It is an awesome thing to be sent by a church to minster. I have been a part of several churches where people were prayed for, sometimes prophesied over, and sent into ministry as missionaries or released into specific ministries locally. I was a part of a church who often prayed over prayer teams who would go pray throughout the city as they walked and prayed and believed God would pour out his Spirit in that area. Sometimes, they would evangelize on the street. Sometimes they would go just before the evening movie was to start. They would pray for anyone in the long ups.

Sometimes, they would preach to those in the long lines ups to popular bars on a Friday or Saturday. Other times, they would walk and pray claiming souls. Literally, the church would be praying and the pastors and elders would lay hands on us and pray that God would use us to pray and evangelize so that Christ would be magnified. They prayed for success but also anointing us with their authority and the church`s authority to accomplish what we were sent to do.

Ritual or Sacrament

A ritual is something people do but it doesn`t necessarily have any power to it. For instance, lighting a candle is something people do as part of worship in many denominations. Its meaning is symbolic only. It had meaning in the Old Testament because God instructed the priests to do it. Bowing one`s head to pray is also a ritual. Many people observe it. The Bible doesn`t say to bow your head and pray. The opposite is true. The Psalmist tells us to lift up our heads to praise God (Psalm 24: 9).

Laying on of hands is not just a religious rite. If you are only completing a ceremony with no faith – there is no sacrament only ritual. The difference between faith filled believers laying hands believing and imparting to believers and those just doing a ritual is huge. It is important that laying on of hands be practiced with faith because it is one of the fundamental doctrines of the Christian Church.

Don`t believe that the laying on of hands without faith will accomplish anything. Also, don`t elevate the laying on of hands of be something it is not. There are certain places it is used. It is not used for everything. Don't believe that you must receive by laying on of hands. It`s one way of receiving. I want to give an example of receiving by faith but still receiving.

Never be Religious

Religious to me means, it must be this way and God can`t do it any other way; I never want to be religious. God can use all kinds of ways to impart to people and to inspire or release people. Years ago, there was a special Evangelist who was preaching at my church during a youth convention. He would evangelize every person he met. He was passionate about reaching souls for Christ. He was inviting us to give our lives radically to God whatever it involved.

As he gave that altar call, I almost ran forward. I felt so strongly that he was personally speaking right into my spirit. I received that call to give myself to Christ wholly. About 1,500 people pressed towards the altar. There wasn`t enough room. People were lined up all up and down the aisles of the church. He was laying hands on some people and praying loudly into the microphone. I was receiving every word he spoke. I was yielding myself to God. I wish I could say he came and laid hands on me – but there were too many people. That doesn't mean I didn't receive something. In fact, I believe, that day, I received a passion for the great commission. It was at that altar I received the baptism of the Holy Spirit as well – with no one laying hands on me. I received whatever God had for me, as much of God as God would give me. I received by faith in God. Never become religious and think, since there was no laying on of hands, nothing happened.

Discipleship and Mentoring

An example of where laying on of hands could be significant could be in a modern church someone is teaching a Bible class and gets an assistant to help him or her. The person trains the assistant so he or she knows what to do, how to do it etc. This exact thing occurred in my life. I was a recent convert, saved about one year. I had been in Bible class with a man nickname Skip and his wife, Polly. They instructed me, poured into me, loved me and were important in my life because I was the only Christian in my family. After the Bible class was over, I wanted to say good bye but it was hard for me. As I started to speak about the end of the semester, Polly, spoke up and said: We want you to come to the next class. I was relieved. I would still get to see them They had become spiritual parents to me. After the second class was complete, Polly approached me and asked me to stay on to help with the class. They got me to help take attendance, get materials, collect money, pray, lead in prayer etc. It was a learning experience because not only was I getting the Bible teaching but I was learning new ways of doing things and soaking up much of the passion for God both Skip and Polly had for God.

What happened is that I became a Bible teacher. I learned how to train others. I have had opportunity both to teach and also to train others for teaching. Imparting of an anointing or mentoring is not with every person you meet. You do it with someone you can spot the gifts in and or someone that God tugs at your heart to train. Not everyone can learn best from me. There is a chemistry between the mentor and the trainee. There is a smooth supernatural relationship where the person is trained and desires to learn all he or she can. You don`t do it casually. You do it prayerfully whether you are the mentor or the trainee. You believe it is God`s best and you give your best effort.

The Bible specifically warns us not to do it casually. It should be done with faith and prayerfully and for a specific purpose. Also, never let just anyone lay hands on you. Guard over this sacrament. Don`t regard it as casual. For example, there may be a class of 70 students; you may notice one or two individuals that have teaching gifts. It is those you should consider on training. It doesn`t mean you care less amount the others. It simply means you are to teach them but perhaps teaching isn`t their main gifting. Someone else should mentor them in some other area of gifting.

The Holy Spirit will use us and speak to us about the individuals. The Holy Spirit will prompt us to invest in those individuals.

1 Timothy 5: 22 Do not lay hands suddenly on anyone, and do not partake of other men's sins. Keep yourself pure.

Also, you don't lay hands and pray for just anyone. As an altar prayer worker, I`ve had the opportunity to pray for hundreds of people who come to the altar for prayer. I would either hold the person`s hand or touch the person on the shoulder or forehead. The people come forward for the purposes of prayer. It was done properly. Should I be mentoring someone, God will quicken to me what to do. My relationship with God is most important. I believe in divine associations. That is, God bring the people; God releases the gift; God instructs about the laying on of hands. It is all Holy Spirit lead. You should never just let anyone lay hands on you and you just never just lay hands on anyone. The reason is because there is an impartation and you don`t just impart to anyone nor do you want just anyone imparting into your life.

Laying on of Hands to Impart a Blessing

The laying on of hands was used by patriarchs in the Old Testament to pronounce generational inherited blessings over the children. In this passage. Jacob, who God called Israel, is praying a blessing on Joseph`s sons Ephraim and Manasseh. He places his right hand on the youngest and his left hand on the oldest. This was not the way blessing were given. Usually, the first born would be prayed for with the right hand on him. Joseph tries to correct Israel but Israel says it is God`s choice not his own. He proclaims the larger blessing on the youngest one.

Genesis 48: 14 Israel stretched out his right hand and laid it on Ephraim's head, who was the younger, and his left hand on Manasseh's head, crossing his hands, for Manasseh was the firstborn.

15 He blessed Joseph and said,

"God, before whom my fathers
    Abraham and Isaac walked,
the God who fed me
    all my life long to this day,
16 the angel who redeemed me from all evil,
    bless the boys;
let them be called by my name,

and the name of my fathers, Abraham and Isaac;
and let them grow into a multitude
　　in the midst of the earth."

17 When Joseph saw that his father laid his right hand on the head of Ephraim, it displeased him, and he took hold of his father's hand to remove it from Ephraim's head to Manasseh's head. 18 Joseph said to his father, "Not so, my father, for this one is the firstborn. Put your right hand on his head."

19 His father refused and said, "I know it, my son, I know it. He will also become a people, and he will also be great, but truly his younger brother will be greater than he, and his descendants will become a multitude of nations." 20 He blessed them that day, saying,

"By you Israel will bless, saying,
　　'May God make you like Ephraim and Manasseh.'"

So he set Ephraim before Manasseh.

　　Israel was about to die so he wanted to pass on the generational blessings of Abraham, Isaac and now Israel – to Joseph's sons. It involved prayer and literal laying on of hands.

Laying on of Hands for Confirmation

　　The opportunity to lay hands on a person to confirm and ground the person in the truths he or she has studied is an essential part of our Christian faith. After studying the doctrines of Christ or after completing elementary teaching on Christian foundations, the students should receive confirmation. I don't know how much this is practiced in the protestant church but it should be.

　　After a nine-month study on the foundations of the Christian faith, we had a special part of the Church service where we went forward for confirmation prayer. The ministers laid their hands on us as we kneeled and they prayed blessings upon us and that we would be firmly rooted in Christ. They prayed that our faith would be strong and that God would quicken the things we had been taught to us so we could live our lives for Christ.

　　We should pray for those who have completed foundational teaching and pray that the participants would be established in the faith. We should pray blessing over them. It not only shows that we approve of their studies but that we (ministers prayed but so did the congregation) receive them and strengthen them in the Christian faith. It is not simply a ritual. There were specific prayers over the different candidates. The person who prayed over me also prophesied over me. It was the leading of the Holy Spirit to establish me in the truths of Christ. They prayed for us to have a firm, strong foundation so we would only build on Christ as our foundation.

Healing

There are many occasions where the disciples laid hands on the sick and they were healed. It was not simply an outward action; it was an impartation of faith for healing. As Paul and his companions were ship wreaked, they came to an Island – it was Malta. Paul lays hands and prays for a person and he is healed.

Acts 28: 8 It happened that the father of Publius lay sick with a fever and dysentery. Paul visited him and, placing his hands on him, prayed and healed him. 9 When this happened, the rest on the island who had diseases also came and were healed.

Our churches should practice the laying on of hands for healing. Often, they will anoint with oil and pray for healing. Believing elders and ministry are often the ones who do it; sometimes altar prayer workers do it. We should offer this sacrament each week so that people who are in need of healing will be able to come. It should be preached from the pulpit regularly so people who are new or who are visiting can get the truth that Jesus Christ is the healer.

Hebrews 13: 8 Jesus Christ is the same yesterday, and today, and forever.

We should be teaching and practicing what the Word of God promises us. Jesus who died for our sins, also took upon Himself all the curses of the law from Deuteronomy 28. The Messiah would fulfill the promises of Isaiah. Jesus Christ is the Messiah.

Isaiah 53: 5 But he was wounded for our transgressions,
    he was bruised for our iniquities;
the chastisement of our peace was upon him,
    and by his stripes we are healed

The words "by his stripes we are healed" means salvation but also physical healing. The Apostle Peter uses these exact words to minister healing (2 Peter 2: 24). It is so important that we pray for one another so there will be no sick among us.

Some people believe the lie that God places sickness on people to teach them or mature them. This is a direct lie that contradicts God 's words. Sickness was named as a curse of sin. God called it a curse. He most certainly would not use a curse to teach one of his children. The truth is some people have not read all of God's Word so if they hear a minister say such a thing as God is in it or some such language, they don't know there is healing. They don't know God.

Deuteronomy 28: 61 Also every sickness and every plague which is not written in the Book of the Law will the Lord bring upon you until you are destroyed.

The blessing of God is on those who serve God and honour Him. If that was true in the Mosaic covenant, it most certainly is true in the covenant of Jesus Christ who paid the full ransom for our lives with his life. Jesus helped show himself as Messiah by healing multitudes of people. If it was God's will to use sickness for those people, Jesus never would have healed them. The good news of the gospel of Jesus Christ means that you can be healed in spirit, soul and body.

Acts 10: 38 how God anointed Jesus of Nazareth with the Holy Spirit and with power, who went about doing good and healing all who were oppressed by the devil, for God was with Him.

Please notice God's Word says the sickness "oppressed by the devil" not a blessing of God.

In Matthew it states the following:

Matthew 12: 15 But when Jesus knew it, He withdrew from there. And great crowds followed Him, and He healed them all,

Since sickness is a curse not a blessing, people may foolishly believe that sickness is a direct result of sin. This is not true. Even the disciples believed that perhaps this was always true. Jesus corrects his disciples and heals the man and clearly says it was not because of sin and he showed God's will to heal.

John 9: 1As Jesus passed by, He saw a man blind from birth. 2 His disciples asked Him, "Rabbi, who sinned, this man or his parents, that he was born blind?"

3 Jesus answered, "Neither this man nor his parents sinned. But it happened so that the works of God might be displayed in him. 4 I must do the works of Him who sent Me while it is day. Night is coming when no one can work. 5 While I am in the world, I am the light of the world."

There are many excellent books on healing and receiving healing. If this is new information to you, please get yourself some Christian materials on healing. There are many present-day healing evangelists such as Oral Roberts, Gloria Copeland, Kenneth Copeland, Marilyn Hickey, Benny Hinn etc. I give you these names because all of them preach Jesus Christ the healer.

Healing comes through faith in Jesus Christ. Faith comes through the hearing of God's Word. It is essential for you to get scriptures about healing into your spirit. Get the scriptures into you by reading them out loud, hearing them and confessing them with your mouth. Reading the Bible and getting God's Word into you is essential for you to be proactive – get the scripture in you so that should something occur and sickness come, you can speak God's word over it and drive it out.

Results of the curse of sin

Sickness, disease, pestilence, hatred, wars, envy, strife – all these things are a result of the curse. Because Adam and Eve sinned, these things exist in our world. You may think God doesn't heal everyone. Please know that if a person is not healed – it is not God who choose to kill him or her. It is essential that we have faith in God's Word yes; it must be on the inside of our innermost being. It is also necessary for us to be wise stewards of our earthly bodies. Please note what we put in to our body directly effects our health.

The Body a Temple

In our modern North American Culture, we often dine on fast food – mostly greasy and salty and high in calories. A can of pop or soda is often 800 calories. A burger sometimes 1,000. Calories. An average person should get 2,500 – 3,000 Calories a day. Junk food –lives up to its name. Chocolate bars, chips, candy – thousands of calories. Please do not pump these things into your body constantly and expect to be healthy. It matters what we put in. I don't pretend to be a dietician, but I made some healthy food choices in my life several years ago because I want to live as long as I can.

1 Corinthians 6: 19 What? Do you not know that your body is the temple of the Holy Spirit, who is in you, whom you have received from God, and that you are not your own? 20 You were bought with a price. Therefore glorify God in your body and in your spirit, which are God's.

Through my explanation, please see that is God's desire for people to live long and be healthy. Also, each person must make wise healthy choices and teach his or her children etc. I have heard of, not witnessed, a miracle of weight loss. Someone overly obese who went for prayer because of all the health issues that arose because of obesity. Although the person was miraculously healed, the person went back to his or her poor habits and became ill once more.

Gloria Copland has an excellent book: Living Long: Finish Strong. It talks about this subject from a Christian point of view. Don't believe the lie that you have to die of a certain disease because it runs in your family. Don't believe the lie that you will die at an early age because others in your family did. Yes we inherit some things from our families, but we can make a difference by doing our part both spiritually building up your faith and naturally by caring for our bodies.

Read the scriptures about healing. Do your part to be healthy but should there be sickness, most certainly get prayer for healing by someone with faith in Jesus the healer.

Matthew 18: 19 "Again I say to you, that if two of you agree on earth about anything they ask, it will be done for them by My Father who is in heaven. 20 For where two or three are assembled in My name, there I am in their midst."

Literally as we pray for each other, Jesus Christ is in the midst of us and His presence can bring healing. The healing can be immediate or gradual. God also gifts doctors and health care professionals to use their skills to help save lives. I have received healing in all these ways. I give God the glory.

Immediate healing

I was not feeling well. I was ill. I believed I could not go to church. My friend came to pick me up as he usually did. I shared with him. He laid hands on me and prayed for me and I was immediately healed. I was able to go to church. It was instant.

Gradual Healing

I have been healed with gradual healing. I was very ill coughing etc. It was hard to breath etc. I read the scriptures to myself. I went to church knowing that they would pray for the sick. I went forward to a minister I knew believing in divine healing. She anointed me with oil and prayed a short prayer over me. I felt God's power go right through the top of my head. I don't know if I expected a longer more awesome prayer or what but as I walked I didn't notice any difference. I shared with my friends that I would have to go home because I wasn't well enough to go out. I believe they were both praying for me. They didn't say they were but I believe it. As I was on my way driving towards home, it suddenly dawned on me; I was breathing normally. I wasn't coughing. I felt excellent. I was healed. I shared it with them and we did our usual special Sunday dinner.

Anointing with oil

James 5: 14 Is anyone sick among you? Let him call for the elders of the church, and let them pray over him, anointing him with oil in the name of the Lord. 15 And the prayer of faith will save the sick, and the Lord will raise him up. And if he has committed any sins, he will be forgiven.

The Bible clearly instructs us what to do if we are ill. We should get elders or ministers to pray the prayer of faith over us for healing anointing us with oil. Oil is only a symbol of the Holy Spirit. There is no special magic about the oil. It is a symbol of God's presence. It reminds the person praying and the receiver to believe for the manifest healing presence of God.

This scripture covers various things. I want to discuss each of them so that your faith rises up for each of them.

1.   Call for the elders – if you cannot get to church, phone and ask someone to come pray for you. You must make a contact with somebody who can pray. You must realize God wants you healthy. Often, I have not only contacted my local church but ministries that I support because they pray and believe for healing.
2.   Anoint with oil in the name of the LORD – The LORD Jesus Christ – anointing with oil is what God commanded we do; we should obey. The oil is a symbol but God said to do it so we should do it.
3.   The prayer of faith will heal the sick. Usually, the ill person needs a boost of faith by someone who is healthy and believes God's Word. It can be the person's own faith; it can be the faith of the minister. Faith must be

present. You cannot pray unscriptural prayers like "If it be your will to heal O God…" and expect results. You will not find a prayer like it in the Bible anywhere. In Luke 5: 12 a leper says those words to Jesus and Jesus says I will heal you. Jesus heals him. A prayer of faith involves praying the scriptures over a person with true faith that impartation for healing is present.
4.   And if he has committed any sins – if the sickness comes because of sin or disobedience to God either neglecting your body or living outside of God's commandments – that is the realm of the curse. God promises, even if the person has sinned, he or she will be forgive as he or she comes for anointing with oil and the healing prayer of faith.

This specific points should comfort any person because God has made provision in this sacrament that you might be healed: spirit, soul and body.

Healing in the soul of a Person

Often people who have experienced the death of a loved one or a divorce or other such tragedy will be overcome with grief. It is normal to grieve the loss of a loved one but we as Christians do not grieve as the world grieves (1 Thessalonians 4: 13). The person who has become wounded in his or her spirit and is overcome with grief not only needs prayer but needs inner healing. Please know the lie that says that healing of such matters comes as years go by. Life may continue but healing doesn't naturally come to a deep wounded in the spirit. The soul of a person is the mind, will and emotions. It is at this level that grief comes. If you are strong in spirit, you can heal in soul. You will overcome the situation.

This is good news for anyone that came from a home where there was abuse or neglect or anything less than a Christian loving family. You don't have to remain a victim. You may have been abused physically, verbally or sexually. You do not have to remain a victim all your life. Do not be given over to self-absorption. If you focus on yourself and what was done to you and why it is unfair etc. you will stay a victim for the remainder of your life. I know it sounds like harsh words, but if you know you are not happy with your life and you are thinking about how you were wounded or you can't see past the divorce or the death, you are in need of healing for your soul. Living in the realm of the soul is never the best for a Christian and it can lead to a wounded spirit.

Galatians 5: 16 I say then, walk in the Spirit, and you shall not fulfill the lust of the flesh.

Galatians 5: 25 If we live in the Spirit, let us also walk in the Spirit.

God wants us to live in the spirit and constantly renew our strength in the Holy Spirit. A broken spirit can occur when a person is constantly living in the soulish realm absorbed with what was done to him or her. This type of person cannot talk about anything without being negative. This type of person is like a black hole to anyone close to him or her. That is the person dumps negative stuff into the atmosphere around him or her. It is not a lack of compassion that causes me to say this. In fact, it is of understanding and compassion of God that compels me to say, no one has to live a victim of life. There is hope in Jesus Christ for healing of your soul.

Isaiah 53: 4 Surely he has borne our grief
   and carried our sorrows;
Yet we esteemed him stricken,
   smitten of God, and afflicted.
5 But he was wounded for our transgressions,
   he was bruised for our iniquities;
the chastisement of our peace was upon him,
   and by his stripes we are healed.

Mere positive thinking will not help a person wounded in the spirit. The person needs deep inner healing of the soul and possibly deliverance of an evil spirit of depression. The good news is that Jesus died for our sins and iniquities and our physical healing but also for our soul. He gave his life as a handsome for our souls. There is provision in the blood of Jesus and in the resurrected LORD for complete and total healing. Jesus took upon himself "the chastisement of our peace" that means he took the curse of all the negative stuff that could ever wound you or I and the curse of it died with Christ; Jesus rose from the dead in triumph over all things of the earth and the curse.

If this describes you or someone close to you, pray for the person yes, but the Word of God must be ministered to the person so he or she knows the truth of Jesus triumph.

John 8: 32 "You shall know the truth, and the truth shall set you free."

Romans 10: 17 So then faith comes by hearing, and hearing by the word of God.

The person should get faith teaching on the healing of the soul. Joyce

Meyer has a strong testimony of complete and total healing and is a living example of this truth that Christ can take a broken person and completely heal and anoint and give new hope and life to a person. She has excellent books and teaching on beauty for ashes, and these topics. I highly recommend her CDs and books be shared with the person in need of inner healing. I have personally known of many people who were transformed by her testimony and her teachings. Once the person acknowledges he or she needs inner healing, the person should get prayer and anointing with oil from a minister of the gospel who believes that Jesus can heal the soul of a person.

I have experienced complete and total healing of my soul. I didn't even know what was going on. I didn't even know about my spiritual condition. I was a Christian, desiring to know God more. At first, I realized I had to come into agreement with God's Word and what God said about me. I started praying and confessing what God says about me. I began to notice my words more and more. The Holy Spirit was so gentle with me, leading me so that I could be transformed and know life beyond any joy I ever knew about. I prayed

Psalm 19: 14 Let the words of my mouth and the meditation of my heart
    be acceptable in Your sight, O Lord, my strength and my Redeemer.

Words we speak

I heard Gloria Copeland preach on God correcting us if we let Him. If we pray " Holy Spirit , please correct my mouth if my words do line up with your word." I prayed it and God started correcting me. If I said something insulting about myself or others, God checked me. Don't say negative things about yourself. You have to live with yourself always. Start saying I can do all things through Christ who strengthens me. Get the word "I can't" out of your vocabulary.

What we Think About

What we think about matters. We can change how we feel depending on what we listen to or what we watch or what we hear. That is why it is so important to get teachings and scriptures to listen to. It is important to watch things that are pure. It is important to think about God's Word and what He says about us in His Word. For instance, God says we are more than conquerors in Christ Jesus. Guard your heart. Keep yourself wholly fixed on God and do not believe anything that goes against what God says in His Word.

Philippians 4: 8 Finally, brothers, whatever things are true, whatever things are honest, whatever things are just, whatever things are pure, whatever things are lovely, whatever things are of good report, if there is any virtue, and if there is any praise, think on these things.

Romans 8: 37 No, in all these things we are more than conquerors through Him who loved us.

Who we are With

Being with someone rather than alone is not always the answer to loneliness. A person who does not build you up spiritually and encourage you with scripture is not someone who can make a difference in your life positively. If the person is not encouraging you spiritually – be alone with God reading the scriptures, listening to them and saying them so your own ears can hear you speak them. What you say about yourself matters the most. If you can get your words in alignment with God's Word, you will start seeing a difference in your life. God will bring Christian friends in your life who will encourage you and strengthen and build you up. Until that occurs, keep constantly build up your own self with psalms and hymns and spiritual songs and scriptures (Ephesians 5: 19).

Jude 1: 20 But you, beloved, build yourselves up in your most holy faith. Pray in the Holy Spirit. 21 Keep yourselves in the love of God while you are waiting for the mercy of our Lord Jesus Christ, which leads to eternal life.

What we do

Give and it shall be given unto you (Luke 6: 38). I know it can mean finances but it can also be a principal of all of life in the spirit. Start serving others. Start giving of yourself to care for others. If you can, get active in your local church by serving or baking at dinners. You could volunteer to start ministering with the Nursing Home Ministries, or teaching a Sunday school class. The principle of the kingdom of God is to give so that you may receive.

I knew of an elderly widow who not only attended all the churches prayer meetings to pray for others but also gave her home life to prayer and intercession for people, for the church for her family etc. If she got a word of God for you in prayer, it most certainly was something to cherish and pray about because she spent most of her life in prayer.

I remember how the more got involved in Church giving, the more I thought about others and less about myself. I saw people in nursing homes, who were dying and who received a bit of joy as I served communion to them or sang hymns with them. The more you serve others, the less you think about yourself.

Prayer for inner healing

The lie is that depressed people need to think about themselves. Just the opposite if true. Those people need to start caring for others. As they serve and give, God honours them by blessing them in so many ways, physically, financially and spiritually.

Receiving a prayer for inner healing is essential for those who have been wounded by life. . It can occur with you and God privately. It can occur with a minister praying for you and anointing you with oil. In order to see a difference in your life, you must make a difference in your life. Start investing the Word of God into your life. Start serving and giving and pursuing God realizing the blessings that God has given to you and becoming thankful. Thank and praise God for what He has done for you. Focus on the blessings not on any negative thing. Focus on the Living Christ who lives in you. If you are living in the Spirit, you cannot live in the flesh. You cannot live in both. Choosing to honour God and to literally believe the Word of God and pray it and confess it and live it – is the answer that can bring a new life.

Jesus laid hands on the Children Imparting a Blessing.

Jesus purposely imparted a blessing on children This was not a mere love for children or an outward sign. It was to impart a blessing. Children were not often considered important but Jesus showed their value by choosing them and using them as an example of simple, true faith.

Matthew 19: 13 Then little children were brought to Him that He might put His hands on them and pray. But the disciples rebuked them.

14 But Jesus said, "Let the little children come to Me, and do not forbid them. For to such belongs the kingdom of heaven." 15 He laid His hands on them and departed from there.

Mark 10: 15 Truly I say to you, whoever does not receive the kingdom of God as a little child shall not enter it." 16 And He took them up in His arms, put His hands on them, and blessed them.

If you are a parent, or have children in your life at all, pray for them. Pray God's blessing on them, protection as well as that they would come to live pleasing lives to God. I believe that parenting is an important responsibility and an awesome privilege because you been entrusted to care for them; spiritually you are the covering over the younger children until they can choose to live for Christ themselves.

My mother not only prayed for us as children but with her grandchildren, she would pray blessings over them each time she bathed them or they came to sit with her. It is a way of passing on a generational blessing of faith. It was especially important because I do not believe the parents prayed for their children. My mother prayed for them; I prayed for them and taught them Bible stories. I invested what I could into those who were in my life.

The Elders and Ministers

Part of what should be occurring in a Church service is that the elders and ministers should be laying hands on people who want a blessing. After I had first become a Christian, I went to every alter call for several years. I would pray about all thing in my life and give myself to God continuously. I have received many blessings by being quick to get prayer. I was the first Christian in my family so the prayers of those people were special to me. I had a Church family that prayed for me. Later, I became a prayer altar worker so that I could pray with others. I delighted in praying over people who came because I knew what God had done for me and believed He could also meet their needs.

Laying on of Hands for Ordination and Separation for Ministry

In Acts 13, Barnabus and Saul are separated for ministry together. The church prayed blessings and protection over them as they were sent out as missionaries. As a pastor or minister is dedicated to the service of God, Other ministers and elders lay hands on them separating them unto God for life long service. The person giving his or her life to serve God in ministry is giving wholly, spirit, soul and body to Jesus Christ for ministry. The ministers praying over them agree and often prophesies come forth because of the faith present.

Laying on of hands for Prophesy

1 Timothy 1: 18 This command I commit to you, my son Timothy, according to the prophecies that were previously given to you, that by them you might fight a good fight, 19 keeping faith and a good conscience, which some have rejected and suffered shipwreck in regard to their faith. 20

The Apostle Paul is reminding Timothy of the prophecies spoken over him. This type of friend is a treasure. A true godly friend will remind you of what God says about you and what prophecies you have received as promises of God. We should continuously remind God of what He has promised us, thanking Him for it and receiving it by faith even before we see a natural manifestation of it.

The gifts of the spirit can be released in a person by laying hands on that person and prophesying and praying in faith. There should be elders and pastors who flow in the prophetic. Apostles and Prophets are usually the ones who get the prophetic words over people but it could come from any of the five-fold ministry. Our part is to receive in faith and stir up the giftings with our prayers and with our words. We can receive callings on God on our life through the laying on of hands with prophesy. What occurs is that something that wasn`t clear suddenly becomes clear and important as the known will of God for your life. Usually. it is a confirmation of something you already know about.

1 Timothy 4: 14 Do not neglect the gift that is in you, which was given to you by prophecy, with the laying on of hands by the elders.

Literally, write the prophecies for yourself and pray them. Say out loud "God I receive this calling..." Literally come into agreement with the prophetic word over your life so that you see it spiritually. Start thanking God for it. Ask the Holy Spirit to direct your steps, and lead you and bring godly doors of opportunity in your life so that you might fulfill the Word of God concerning your life.

Minister's Candidate school

After three years of studying for ministry, we were to receive the laying on of hands with prophesy. My pastor was a strong prophet of God who usually prayed over all the graduates and prophesied over them, In my class, he did not do it as usual. He delayed it for a year. He gathered together several known prophets of God who would all lay hands on us and prophesy over us. This was something I longed for. It was the culmination of my studies. It meant a blessing over my life. I fasted. Please know this is a big deal for me. Fasting and prayer should be a part of our Christian lifestyle, but it comes easier to some than others. I was so expectant of what God would say about me through the prophets. I was also nervous. I kept in prayer all the way to church and the service itself was charged with an atmosphere of faith for the prophetic. Gathering the prophets is a special atmosphere. If you have not experienced it, I highly recommend you get into a true prophet of God's service. There is a special atmosphere for receiving miracles from God. I had studied three years of ministry classes, given myself to prayer and to serving in the Church. I wanted that special blessing that would come believing God would use those ministers to speak words of blessing over me.

In our graduating class, the ministers called each one of us up to the altar and we kneeled as the different prophets prayed and prophesied over us. They recorded each person's prophetic word so that we could remember and as proof so we could know what to pray for. I highly recommend that you get a tape or a cd or mp3 of the prophecy as proof not only for your own self but as proof against any lie that may try to rise against it. I have kept those prophecies throughout the years and treasured them. I prayed them. I thank God for them. They have been like a compass to help me understand the seasons and help me to follow Christ.

Not just any person should lay hands on you. It should be somebody you respect, somebody you know, somebody who is true and sincere; the motives of the person's heart matter. God will use prophets and apostles of God to prophesy and pray over those who believe to receive from the laying on of hands with prophesy. Faith is a key ingredient on your part and on the ministry team's part.

9 CONCLUSION

It is my prayer that my book on the sacraments will be a blessing to you so that as you celebrate the stones of remembrance God has given us by way of the sacraments, you will be encouraged, quickened to receive from God in them and be stirred with desire to share these truths with others.

Prayer of Salvation

Lord Jesus, I confess I need a Saviour. I believe you died on the cross, rose from the dead and ascended into heaven and that you are coming back again. I believe with my heart and confess with my mouth that you Lord Jesus Christ are my Saviour and LORD. Thank you for your blood shed for me. I desire to live for you for all of my life. O God teach me to understand the Bible; instruct me and teach me. Help me to find a local church where I can receive teaching and preaching that will help me to grow in the faith. Holy Spirit, direct my steps and lead me as I live for Christ. Amen.

Prayer for Receiving the Baptism of the Holy Spirit

Thank you Holy Spirit for your abiding presence; that you live in me. You clearly said if we would repent and be baptized in the name of Jesus, we would receive the gift of the Holy Spirit. Jesus, I want you to baptize me in the Holy Spirit with the evidence of speaking in other tongues. I want all of you that you will give me. God I offer myself I living sacrifice, spirit, soul and body. Come fill me to overflowing. I believe the gifs of the Spirit are given to all who are believers in Jesus. Amen.

INSTRUCTION: NOW START PRAISING GOD IN YOUR NATURAL LANGUAGE AND KEEP PRAISING GOD THANKING HIM FOR THE GIFT OF THE HOLY SPIRIT. YOU WILL FEEL A BUBBLING UP ON THE INSIDE OF YOU. SPEAK THE WORDS THE HOLY SPIRIT GIVES YOU.

Prayer for Partaking in the Sacraments

O God, I thank you for the sacrament of NAME IT . Come Holy Spirit and reveal Christ to me through your presence and my faith in you. Amen

OTHER BOOKS BY CHRIS A. LEGEBOW

Available on Amazon.ca Amazon.com or Amazon.ca or Kindle Or the Create Space webstore.

Living Word Publishers

An Excellent Spirit: Living Life Wholly Unto God

Covenant With God: God's Relationship With Man

Discovering and Using your Spiritual Gifts

Kinds of Prayer. Knowing Them and Using Them Effectively

Living Life Fully: Knowing your Purpose

The Anointing: the Glory of God

The High Calling: Life Worth Living

The Sacraments: A Charismatic Guide

ABOUT THE AUTHOR

Chris Legebow is a Christian Professor of English and Communications. She has taught at the elementary, high school and College and University levels. She has ministered in her local churches in intercessory prayer, teaching Sunday school and other Christian Doctrine classes to children and youths. She has preached to congregations and given her testimony. Although she was not raised in a Christian home, she came to know Jesus Christ as her Saviour and LORD while she was studying in University. This radically transformed her life in terms of priorities and commitment. She has a strong passion for the great commission – that Jesus Christ would be preached throughout all the earth believing that it a major sign of the LORD's return. She has been a part of several different types of full gospel charismatic churches but has also gained much of her insight and enlightenment from Christian Media and broadcasting. She hopes to continue ministering, serving, interceding and giving and teaching until the LORD returns.

www.ingramcontent.com/pod-product-compliance
Lightning Source LLC
Chambersburg PA
CBHW020507030426
42337CB00011B/266